If Only You Would Ask

If Only You Would Ask

Praying God's Conditional Promises

Ronnie W. Rogers

Foreword by Mark H. Ballard

RESOURCE *Publications* • Eugene, Oregon

Resource Publications
An Imprint of Wipf and Stock Publishers
199 W. 8th Ave., Suite 3
Eugene, OR 97401

www.wipfandstock.com

PAPERBACK ISBN: 978-1-6667-3743-1
HARDCOVER ISBN: 978-1-6667-9687-2
EBOOK ISBN: 978-1-6667-9688-9

MARCH 25, 2022 8:24 AM

I dedicate this book to the best two sons-in-law a father could ask for. Rocky Heinrich is the husband of our eldest daughter and father to four of our grandchildren, three boys and one girl. J. R. Crosby is the husband of our youngest daughter and father of three of our grandsons. Rocky and J. R. have proven themselves to be men of spiritual integrity by providing godly love and direction for my daughters and grandchildren. For such men we did pray, and God has graciously granted in each of them even more than we ever expected.

Beyond this, they have shown the utmost love, respect, and honor to Gina (my wife) and me, all of which make us rich beyond measure. I pray God's promises to answer prayers, build your faith, and strengthen your trust and dependence on him as you lead your families to follow Christ regardless of the cost.

Contents

Foreword

It was a Sunday morning in 2011, nearly two years after I resigned from serving as the Senior Pastor of Christian Fellowship Baptist Church in Londonderry, NH. Cindy and I had stepped out in faith and obedience to the Lord's call to launch a Baptist College in New England. While Cindy helped our son, Benjamin, get ready to go to church on my last day as the pastor, I added up the money in my savings account, my checking account, and all the money in my pocket. The total came to forty-seven dollars. Of course, we also had enough food in the refrigerator and cabinets to last a little more than a week and a tank full of gas in the truck. There was no promise of ever receiving a paycheck again, but we had the assurance that our Lord would never call us to do something and then let us starve. So, trusting in his provision, we simply made our requests known unto him. Day after day, our amazing Lord faithfully provided.

For nearly two years, we watched as the Lord repeatedly came through time after time. Sometimes he would move on someone's heart to fill the gas tank of our truck. Sometimes we would open the door to the truck and find a couple of bags of groceries. Occasionally someone would hand me some cash and say, "This money is not for the college, but for you, Cindy, and Ben." Other times it was a gift card, or someone would take us out to dinner. No matter how the Lord provided day by day, it was always clear that it came from the Father's hand. Like David, we learned to say, "The Lord is my shepherd, I shall not want" (Ps 23:1, KJV). We would pray, asking the Lord to provide, and he did! It was an amazing journey.

Yet, on this particular Sunday in 2011, it seemed as though the provision had come to an end. I had an assignment to preach at Exeter Community Church in Exeter, NH. We lived fifty-six miles away in Allenstown,

NH. I had no money. Our vehicle got twelve to fifteen miles to the gallon, and the gas tank had less than one gallon in it.

All evening on Friday and all day on Saturday, I expected that at any moment, the Lord would send someone by the house to give us some money. This would allow me to put gas in the tank and keep my preaching appointment on Sunday. No one came by Friday evening. We stayed home all day Saturday, waiting on the Lord to provide the gas needed the following day. When we went to bed on Saturday night, we were still waiting. Nothing came.

I looked up at the clock, and it was time to leave for Exeter. I thought, if there was some way I could drive the fifty-six miles, maybe someone at the church would give me enough cash to gas up and get home. I knew there was no way to go fifty-six miles when the gas I had would not even get me ten miles down the road. The moment of truth had arrived. Did I really believe that I could pray, asking God to get us to Exeter and that he would respond to my prayer? Or, should I call the pastor, apologize, and stay home? If I did go, should I take Cindy and Ben? What if we ran out on the way, and I had to walk for help? Maybe I should have them stay home.

Walking out to the car, I half expected someone to show up and provide the money. No one came. Cindy, Ben, and I got into the truck. I turned the key, and the motor fired up. I didn't tell Cindy that we could not go more than ten miles on the gas we had. There was no reason for both of us to worry. Then it dawned on me I shouldn't worry either. So, I prayed silently. "Father, you gave me this preaching assignment, for which I am grateful. However, you and I both know that I don't even have enough gas to get three-fifths of the way to Exeter. Lord, you promised to meet our needs. Please do something to get us to Exeter. Help me to trust you and just drive."

I pulled out of the driveway and started down the road. We passed the mile mark, then the five-mile mark. Soon, we passed ten miles. I expected the motor to die at any moment. I began to worry. I returned to silent prayer. "Lord, you caused the widow's oil and flour to never run out when she provided a meal for Elijah. Surely, you can cause me not to run out of gas. Please get us to Exeter." Soon we crossed the fifteen-mile mark. Before long, twenty miles had gone by, then thirty, then forty. As we neared the church, I began to believe that we would make it. Soon we turned into the parking lot where the church met.

I dropped Cindy off at the front door and parked in the back of the lot. After shutting off the key, I paused to thank Jesus for doing what was impossible. I then said, "You did an amazing thing to get us here. Now, please let the church give me a stipend for preaching and cause them to give it in cash, lead someone to give me cash, or offer to fill my gas tank." With that settled, Ben and I walked to the front of the building and entered just in time for the service to begin.

After a wonderful time of singing, prayer, and Scripture reading, the pastor introduced me to share a report about the progress toward launching Northeastern Baptist College, scheduled to open in 2013. After a brief update, I led the congregation in prayer and then preached the morning message. Following the worship service, the pastor told us that the church had prepared a meal to share with us. We ate, fellowshipped, and answered additional questions about launching the college in 2013. Soon, everyone began to leave, but no one gave me a cash gift, and no one offered to fill the gas tank.

We made our way out to the truck, and just as I was getting in, the pastor came out to the parking lot waving at me. As he stepped to the driver's side window, he handed me an envelope. My heart leaped as I anticipated the Lord had answered my prayers. We visited a moment, and he turned to leave. I reached into my pocket, where I had put the envelope. As I opened it, I could see there was no cash. Instead, there was a check for fifty dollars. There was no place I could cash this check on a Sunday. I bowed my head again and asked the Lord to provide a way for me to get home. I turned the key, and to my amazement, the truck started. I pulled up to the door, picked up Cindy, and started home.

After traveling about twenty miles down the road, I saw a gas station. I pulled in and just sat there a minute. I asked Cindy if she had any money, to which she replied that she had given me all she had a couple of weeks earlier.

I then prayed again. "Father, you know I have already driven seventy-six miles today on ten miles worth of gas. I don't know why you haven't provided money, but you kept us going this far. Please help us to get home. Then tomorrow morning, I need you to get me to the bank to cash this check and on to a gas station, all without running out of gas. Lord, I believe you can do this. It is not hard for you. But Lord, I struggle to know if you will. Lord, I believe, but please help my unbelief. In Jesus' name, Amen." As

I pulled back onto the highway, I began to sing "I Just Keep Trusting My Lord."[1]

With every passing mile, I prayed more intently. Soon I found myself turning into our driveway. We had driven 112 miles on ten miles worth of gas. The next morning, I got in the truck, drove another ten miles to the bank, sat in the drive-through line, cashed the check, and drove another five miles. Pulling up to the gas pump, I shut off the truck, stepped out, and filled the tank. Altogether we had driven a little over 127 miles on just enough gas to go ten miles.

This event raises several questions.

1. Did the Father perform this miracle in response to my prayer, or was this simply his will to do so from the beginning and my prayer was of no consequence?

2. Did the Father prompt me to pray and then somehow use my prayers?

3. If I had chosen not to pray, would I have made it to Exeter, home, to the bank, and then to the gas station?

4. Could God have said "no" to my prayers, or was he obligated to act?

5. How does prayer relate to man's free will, Calvinism, God's sovereignty, and God's will?

6. If our prayers really do make a difference, how is God still sovereign?

7. If our prayers do not make a real difference, why pray at all?

Rarely does any believer stop to give serious consideration to such questions. Yet, if prayer does not really change things, what is the point of praying? I suspect that questions like these have hindered the prayer life of many believers. Some simply throw up their hands and give up on prayer. Others pray but never really expect their prayers to change anything. Few are brave enough to give serious consideration to these questions. If they do consider these difficult questions, they are likely to keep them to themselves.

Today, it is my privilege to commend to you the excellent work you hold in your hands. Ronnie Rogers has once again written a clear-thinking monograph that refuses to shy away from the tough questions. The reader will be challenged to think deeply about prayer. The questions asked above, along with a host of other such questions, are examined directly. The thoughtful and prayerful reader will ultimately learn from this book, be

1. Peterson, "I Just Keep Trusting."

challenged to reconsider their beliefs and practices regarding prayer, and will become a more effective prayer warrior for the glory of the Lord.

Thank you, Ronnie Rogers, for asking the questions others will not! Thank you for taking a hard look at prayer. Thank you for your thoroughly biblical treatment of the topic. May the Father use this book to raise up prayer warriors who understand the urgency of the hour!

Mark H. Ballard, PhD
President/Founder, Northeastern Baptist College
Bennington, VT

Introduction

ALTHOUGH PRAYER IS CENTRAL to the Christian life, it does contain some confusing elements as well. I will seek to help us overcome some of the more confusing elements that discourage us from praying as we should. The confusion arises from a deep sense of not understanding how prayer really can change me, others, things, and events or outcomes in light of the biblical teachings on subjects like God's sovereignty, "Your will be done," predestination, and God's foreknowledge. To say it another way, if God is sovereign, his will is singular, best, and always done, and we are to pray for God's will to be done, then why make our requests known to him or even pray, other than to pray "Your will be done." You might say, well, Scripture commands us to pray. While that is true, the commands and instructions to pray do not seem to be commands for the sake of giving a command. They give every indication of telling us to pray because some things will be different if we pray. Specifically, Scripture connects the reception of many of God's promises to whether or not we ask or pray so that asking and prayer really make a difference in many outcomes.

The confusion arises because of seemingly competing ideas. On the one hand, "Your will be done" is often presented or understood to imply that there is what we pray and ask for (our requests), and then there is God's will; unless we are praying in concert with what *he has already predetermined to happen*, our requests are not according to his will, and, therefore, should not and will not be answered. Such tends to move us toward asking ourselves, albeit ever so privately, why make my requests known if I am going to pray for God's will, which is going to happen regardless if I pray or I don't pray?

On the other hand, Scripture calls for passionate and earnest prayer (Luke 22:44; 1 Thess 3:10; Jas 5:17), praying "at all times" (Eph 6:18), "pray without ceasing" (1 Thess 5:17), "for all things" (Phil 4:6), not losing heart (Luke 18:1), prayer with fasting (Acts 13:3), asking for specific things (Jas 1:5), and that we need protections by "praying in the Holy Spirit" (Jude 20). Add to this: God answers prayer (Isa 37:15–21; Matt 7:7; John 16:23–24; 14:13–14; Jas 4:2; 5:16–18; 1 John 5:14–15).

If Scripture taught *either* God's sovereignty, foreknowledge, predestination, and "Your will be done" *or* the call to pray for everything by making our requests known through praying passionately and unceasingly coupled with his repeated promises to answer our prayers, we would not be confused. But it is the biblical teaching of *both* that leads to our confusion and lack of consistent prayer.

Before we can understand prayer in which we are commanded to make our requests known with God's promises to answer our requests in light of his sovereignty, predestination, foreknowledge, man's free will, and what it means to pray in the will of God, we have to understand a few things. We will need to know something about the nature of both God and man, the nature of making choices, how it is that our choices matter, and what is comprehended (included) in the phrase "Your will be done." Then we will be ready to appreciate the strategic place of prayer in the life of a believer.

I will briefly lay out the main ideas in these areas without offering a detailed defense or a look into the in-depth reasoning for my conclusions because that would detract from my intent to make this a practical and readable book about prayer while integrating some deep and invaluable truths of Scripture. If you are interested in the deeper aspects of my explanations, definitions, and reasoning found in this book, you can read about them in my book, *Does God Love All or Some? Comparing Biblical Extensivism and Calvinism's Exclusivism.*

The following principles should guide our prayers:

1. We should always desire that all our prayers glorify God.

2. We should always demonstrate the utmost trust in God.

3. We should always make our requests known to God.

4. We should understand that praying in God's will includes making our requests known to God.

5. We should pray, knowing some things will be different if we pray than if we do not pray.

— 6. "Your will be done" cannot be substituted for an authentic heart request to our heavenly Father.

I truly pray God will use the truths in this book to help everyone who reads it to pray like never before. The transformation can be one from guilt over a lack of passionate prayer to a life of normal, passionate prayer. It will be a transformation from confused praying to clear praying. This new passionate and clear prayer life comes about by having a better understanding of how praying for specific requests is in perfect harmony with God's sovereignty, predestination, foreknowledge, man's free will, and the need to pray desirously for the Lord's will to be done.

Acknowledgments

MOST OF ALL, I thank Jesus for the work he has done in my life. I thank Gina, my wife, confidant, friend, and co-laborer in life and ministry, who has made the greatest impact upon my life other than Jesus.

I thank Larry Toothaker and Billy Wolfe for their gracious willingness to proof my manuscript and provide invaluable insights; Anita Charlson for her tireless and professional editing of this manuscript; Gina Rogers, Carol Ann Lindley, and Bill Smith for their invaluable assessment of the book, J. R. Crosby for his excellent cover design and insights; Trinity's elders for their unwavering support of my commitment to study and their steadfast encouragement to equip the saints and write; as well as my brothers and sisters in Trinity Baptist Church whom I have been blessed beyond measure to serve for twenty-three years. You have loved me without measure and provided me the greatest opportunity for spiritual growth. My longevity as your pastor is a testimony of your Christlike gracious and generous forbearing love towards me. No man could deserve such a life of being loved, but none so little as me.

I will live and die indebted to all of you for your love and support.

1

Why We Might Not Pray as We Should

I DO NOT MEAN to discount the reasons others write about for not praying, such as the flesh, weak faith, or sin in a person's life, but I would like to add some prayer discouragers that do not seem to be sufficiently addressed. I would also like to resolve them so that rather than being discouragers to prayer, they become encouragers.

There are many reasons why we as Christians do not pray as we should, but there are also many great resources to address the normal reasons Christians fail to pray as we should. This book is not trying to replace those, but rather, I pray, contribute to encouraging Christians to pray. I seek to address some of the lesser spoken of belief issues that hinder passionate and consistent prayer. This chapter suggests some of the thoughts, questions, and considerations that can discourage prayer; we will seek to clear them up in the remainder of the book. To summarize what this book will address, consider the following:

- If God is in sovereign control of everything, and if he is omniscient (foreknows the future), how can our prayers change things? How can we change tomorrow by praying if God already knows what is going to happen tomorrow? Would that not make God wrong, or at least in a position of having to learn from our prayers?

- If our prayers are meaningful in the sense that they change events, how can God be sovereign? If there are almost eight billion people on earth, and Christians are offering up hundreds of thousands of prayers to change things, how can God eternally know the future; how can he be sovereign over a future that is changed by the prayers of his people?

◻ If we are to pray for God's will to be done (Matt 6:10), and if God's will is set from eternity (Eph 1:11), then why should we think our prayers can change anything? If God's will is perfect, can we change that, and if we did, would that make it a less perfect will?

◻ If God's will is perfect, and it is, do we even want to change it?

◻ Since we must pray, "Your will be done," and his will is most assuredly going to be done, what is the point of making our requests known to God? Should we not just pray "Your will be done" and be done with it?

In light of these thoughts, it is understandable why we struggle to be passionate about making our requests known to God. When we just think about the biblical teaching that prayer changes things and events, we do OK Conversely, when we think about God, who knows everything and is working everything according to his divine plan, we are OK But when we think about how those two realities work together, confusion abounds. And this confusion can hinder our prayer life, which is closely followed by the partner to a weak prayer life, which is a cold and distant relationship with God. Focusing too much on the power of prayer to change things will diminish our respect and understanding of God's sovereignty and will. Focusing too much on God's divine immutable will and sovereignty will erode our belief in the essentialness of prayer, as far as being able to walk with God and see changes in outcomes from our prayers.

Not understanding how these two realities work together is a prayer killer, finally arriving at praying out of believing that whether I pray or do not pray, things will work out according to God's sovereign will. Although we continue to pray out of obedience because we are told to pray (Matt 6:9–15), we do so hoping it will help in some way. As we say, you can always pray even if you cannot do anything else. Sometimes involving that if we can do something else, we should prioritize that over prayer.

We agree that God is sovereign, God knows all things, and God is in control, which are all true. But what do they mean concerning prayer, and particularly in the area of the Bible's conditional promises? A conditional is a statement or command made with a stated or implied corresponding dependent outcome. The outcome is based on meeting the condition. For example, Jesus said, "Whatever you ask in My name, that will I do" (John 14:13). The condition is to ask in Jesus' name, and the outcome or promise is that if you ask, he will do what you ask. Quite commonly, but not always, "if" identifies conditionals or if not by the word "if," by the idea of "if." Another example of a conditional is Matt 6:14, which says, "For if you forgive others for their transgressions, your heavenly Father will also forgive you." The Father's forgiveness of us is conditioned on whether or not we forgive others. When Scripture calls on humans to choose between options with corresponding consequences, that is a conditional.

While comfort surely is derived from such beliefs as God's sovereignty and omniscience, these beliefs can also leave us confused about how prayer fits in with these great truths, which leaves us with a less passionate prayer life; at least we are not praying with a strong belief that our prayers matter in how things develop or end up. Further weakening of our prayer life often takes place when we pray for something, and nothing happens, or even worse, things go from bad to dreadful. After that happens a few times, even if we do not say it out loud, we can begin to wonder if our prayers matter. We may also begin to question if prayer can truly change an event or outcome. Meaning, will the outcome of what I pray about be different if I pray than if I had not prayed at all? If so, how, and how will I know? Are there things we cannot change with prayer? If so, how can we know them?

The Holy Spirit commands us, "So then do not be foolish, but understand what the will of the Lord is" (Eph 5:17). To which, we all can say a hearty amen! But the nagging questions that come on the heels of our amen are: Where does prayer fit in with the will of the Lord? What about all the areas that Scripture does not speak to directly? How do Scriptures that tell us to pray specifically, which clearly either imply or even explicitly state that outcomes depend on our praying, matter in light of God's sovereign will?

Paul tells us, "With all prayer and petition pray at all times" (Eph 6:18a). Every other aspect of preparation for spiritual warfare outlined in Eph 6:10–21 has a specific protective element to it. But the instruction to pray seems to be a general directive that permeates all areas of protection and spiritual armor and warfare. Then, in the next verse, Paul personally requests prayer saying, "pray on my behalf" (Eph 6:19a). As Paul has done, we also request others to pray on our behalf. But do we pray for others as though their life, or ours, will be different if we pray than if we do not pray, believing Mark 11:23–24? You know, how does praying for someone matter in light of the truth that "also we . . . having been predestined according to His purpose who works all things after the counsel of His will" (Eph 1:11)?

Think about this specific prayer request of Paul. "And pray on my behalf, that utterance may be given to me in the opening of my mouth, to make known with boldness the mystery of the gospel, for which I am an ambassador in chains; that in proclaiming it I may speak boldly, as I ought to speak" (Eph 6:19–20). This specific request raises the question, could the prayers of the Ephesians really have impacted the spread of the gospel? Could their prayers have impacted people hearing the gospel and even being saved? That is to say, would Paul's spreading of the gospel have been different or even more effective if the Ephesians prayed than it would be if they did not pray?

We find this kind of emphasis on prayer making a difference throughout Scripture, but, again, how do we reconcile this with "Your will be done," other people having free will, and the outcome of the gospel encounter (Matt 26:42)? What if Jesus had not prayed for the disciples (John 17:13–19), for those who heard the gospel through them, and those who came after them, which includes us? He prayed "so that the world may believe that you sent me" (John 17:20–21). What if he had not prayed for us and the unsaved of our day? Would lives have turned out differently? And if it does have an effect, how does it work?

Further confusing these issues is the teaching known as Calvinism. While I will explain these concepts in chapters 3 and 4, I mention them here preliminarily since they are relevant to this chapter and chapter 2.

Calvinism claims that God decreed (foreordained or predetermined) everything and gave man compatible moral freedom, meaning there is nothing man can do to change anything because God predetermined everything, and man cannot override that. This perspective raises the question, what possible difference can prayer make in what God has determined it to be, whether it was Paul beseeching the Ephesians to pray or Jesus praying for others? If Calvinism is true, then the truth is none of these prayers make a difference in the way things turn out, even though it seems that Jesus chose to pray, and Paul chose to implore the Ephesians to pray for the precise purpose of changing outcomes to be different than if they did not pray.

There is no indication that either Jesus or Paul understood their choice to pray as a determined event in which they could not have chosen otherwise. In an attempt to reconcile Scripture's conditional statements with Calvinism's determinism, Calvinists often say prayer and the words prayed are a part of the process. But within Calvinism, whether one prays or not, including the very words prayed, the prayer and words are as determined as everything else, and any thought that a person could choose to act differently than he did is a delusion. 〉

But Scripture portrays prayer undeniably differently. Scripture teaches that prayer, at least some of the time, results in different outcomes than if the person did not pray, and that the person chose to pray that specific prayer because he wanted a different outcome than the one happening or about to happen. He was not predetermined to pray, and he did not see the event he was praying about as determined. I believe a normal reading of Scripture, particularly the passages depicting human interaction with each other or with God, God's promises, conditional statements, and prayer, along with much of the language employed, becomes nonsensical and even misleading if a person is consistent with Calvinism's belief that everything is decreed in unconditional election and compatible moral freedom.[1] Calvinism, therefore, by its actual nature, reduces most of the normal language of Scripture depicting people making choices between accessible options with their comparable encouragements and warnings to utterly meaningless gibberish to maintain their view that God determines everything.

I believe there are accessible options in contrast to the hypothetical options of Calvinism. By accessible options, I mean, given the same past and circumstances, the same person could choose one option over another, and whatever he did choose to do, he could have chosen differently in the very same situation—libertarian free will. You chose to read this book at this time, but you could have chosen not to. Whereas hypothetical options mean that if something (such as the person's past, determined desires, or timing) was different, he could have chosen differently. Thus, the hypothetical, in contrast to accessible options, still means that in the moral moment of decision (without having a different past which he did not have), the person could still not have actually chosen differently. That is to say, you chose to read this book, but you could not have actually chosen not to read this book at this time.

---

1. See Appendix 1 for a fuller explanation of why this is true in Calvinism. Unconditional election is the doctrine of Calvinism that teaches God was pleased to choose some to be saved and equally pleased to not provide salvation for others; the latter are known as the non-elect and reprobates. I often use the adjective *consistent* when referring to Calvinism. I do so because while what I am saying is reflective of consistent Calvinism, Calvinists often speak in ways that are inconsistent with the non-negotiables of Calvinism and by doing so they seem to make what I am saying to not be reflective of Calvinism, but it is.

I am writing this book from the perspective of what I call Extensiv-
..m. Generally speaking, I use Extensivism instead of non-Calvinism and
Extensivists for non-Calvinists.[2] Extensivism believes God endowed man
with libertarian moral freedom (free will). Libertarian freedom or free
will says that humans can choose to act or refrain in some situations, and
whatever they chose to do, they could have chosen differently even with
the same past. A person's past can influence their choice, as can many other
things, but it does not determine their choice. The person choosing does
that because he has agency.

It is easy to see that libertarian free will says that determinism and
moral responsibility are not compatible, even though libertarianism recognizes that some things are determined by God apart from human influence.
However, in many cases, humans have a choice. As an Extensivist, I believe
people can make choices which change some outcomes to be different than
if they would have chosen differently. So that in some areas of life, things
or outcomes will turn out differently if a person decides to pray than if they
did not. This reality is only because God desired his plan to include some
things to be the result of libertarian freewill choice of humans that he created in his image; they can choose one option over another, and whatever
they choose, they could have chosen differently. Consequently, prayer can
really change outcomes. Even though libertarian free will makes sense of
the countless events in Scripture where people choose between options,
and prayer changes outcomes, it still leaves the question of how that fits
with God's eternally conceived plan, praying in God's will, praying "Your
will be done" and his knowing everything. Prayerfully, we will answer that
in the remainder of this book.

These considerations bring us back to this truth. If the Bible presented
predestination, foreknowledge, and God working everything "after the
counsel of His will" (Eph 1:11), or that our choices and prayers could affect
the outcome of some things if a person chose differently or did not pray
(Jas 5:13–18), there would be no confusion. The problem arises because
the Bible presents both of these truths throughout the Scripture. But how
can God work everything according to his sovereign will, and yet different
results or outcomes occur if someone prays than if they did not pray? If
they pray for a result, and it happens; could that be proof that it was in the
will of God? But what if the same person does not pray, and the outcome is
different than if he had prayed? Can that also be the will of God? If so, how?

2. See Authorial Glossary for a fuller definition.

Consider the following three questions in light of God's sovereignty and eternal foreknowledge, which means God has always exhaustively known everything. Humanly speaking, more than a trillion billion years ago, God knew that you would be reading this book and what you would think about it. Consider these questions:

1. Does prayer change something (an event) to take place differently than it would have had I not prayed? Can you pray about a meeting on Friday so that what happens in the meeting is different than it would have been had you not prayed? Or if I do not pray and my marriage falls apart, could we have worked things out if I had prayed?

2. Can prayer *affect* or influence other persons who may be unaware of our prayers on their behalf? Can prayer change a person in a way he does not want to be changed? What about the teenager who is in rebellion? Or an unfair employer who does not want to change? Conversely, can others praying for you affect you so that you change in ways that you did not initially desire or may not desire even now? It's great to think about changing the people around us, but we do not want to think about someone changing us through prayer, at least in a way we are not desirous to be changed.

   If our prayers can accomplish changing other people, that raises questions about free will. Libertarian free will means a person can choose between various options, and that choice makes a difference in the outcome. What if our prayer is contrary to what the person we are praying for wants to do by exercising his free choice? We pray all the time for friends or family we love. But can our prayers influence them if they have free will? And then what about things that are predestined? And how do we know what is predestined and what is not?

3. Can prayers *cause* a person with free will to change what they would have done without the prayers? Here, we are talking about a causal relationship between our prayers and another person's actions rather than just influencing someone as in the previous consideration. Would that not mean we are controlling their free will or that they are controlling ours? We seldom have a problem with our prayers controlling others; an unruly child or someone who means us harm comes to mind. But we are not so accommodating when we think of others' prayers controlling us! The truth is, we often pray for children, spouses, friends, and employers; we do so with the idea that our

prayers can at least influence the situation, but often we are content to cause circumstances that change their choices. But my question is, is there ever really a causal relationship between our prayer and another person's action without eliminating the free will of others?

These are the types of disturbing questions and seemingly unresolvable deterrents to passionate prayer I seek to resolve. If we are going to pray, what are the real reasons? What is our motivation? Knowing that we are commanded to pray should be enough (Matt 6:9), but when we seriously consider God's sovereignty, predestination, foreknowledge, and man's free will, confusion arises. While that confusion does not diminish our belief in prayer, for those of us who believe the Bible, it can seriously reduce our passion for and practice of prayer. Such confusion can result in a less than biblical prayer of robust faith (Mark 11:24; Jas 5:15). We then live a Christian life of believing in the concept of prayer without the consistent and passionate practice of prayer. This confusion can lead us to just trusting God to do whatever he is going to do, "Your will be done," rather than recognizing he has planned for our prayers to play a vital role in what he desires to do.

2

Three Reasons to Pray

WHEN PEOPLE SPEAK OF prayer or teach on prayer, they often give different reasons for praying. Sometimes the teacher will say prayer is to conform us to God's will, which, if left alone, either minimizes or negates the idea that prayer changes outcomes. This perspective is often promoted by Calvinists and some Extensivists who do not understand the full implications of the statement. For if everything is determined, nothing exists that prayer can change, even though some determinists mistakenly say prayer can change our attitude or perspective. However, technically, the person's attitude and outlook are determined like everything else, so even that cannot be changed by prayer in an undetermined way. For those who believe everything is determined, the one who prays and even the words he prays and the one who does not pray are equally determined, and so are their attitudes about prayer.

Others highlight the relational aspect of prayer. This viewpoint emphasizes fellowship with God. Still, others focus more on what God will do in response to prayer, so the emphasis is the power of prayer to change outcomes.

If a person overemphasizes any one of these, it creates a somewhat disharmonious relationship between the three. The various perspectives on prayer run the full spectrum from the Calvinist perspective that everything is determined so that prayer cannot actually change anything to be different than what God eternally determined to the Word of Faith perspective, which teaches we can create our own reality by believing strongly enough. The determinist perspective is often difficult to detect since they frequently speak with language more suitable for those who believe in libertarian free will. The Word of Faith perspective can extend to man being able to create realities like God. In reality, all three emphases contain some truth, which means, properly understood, they work together seamlessly.

The way to start our journey toward a passionate and consistent prayer life is by resolving the paradoxes between God's sovereignty, man's libertarian free will, and prayer as presented in the Bible, but this requires understanding the following. The Bible presents *some* things as predetermined. These events (outcomes) are not affected by man's choice or prayer; they are predestined by God and cannot be changed. These are known as definite events. Because they are determined, they happen necessarily. Some biblical examples are God creating the universe, the birth of Christ, and God designating a time in which he will judge every sin (Rev 20:11–15). No act, choice, or prayer of man can alter these kinds of events. These things are unaffected by human involvement.

The Bible also presents some things as undetermined. God has designed these events (outcomes) so that they are affected by man's choices or prayers. As a result, the outcome is different than if the person had chosen differently or had not prayed. The decisions or acts of libertarian free beings are known as contingencies since their existence is contingent on human choice. A contingency (the human choice that did not have to happen) creates an event known as an indefinite event because it may or may not happen depending on the person's choice. Therefore, the event happens certainly (God omnisciently knows what will happen) and not necessarily because it is not determined to happen apart from human influence. Indefinite events are uncertain to humans since we cannot know it will happen until it does, but they are certain to happen in the mind of God.

Often these indefinite events are the result of what we call a conditional. Remember, a conditional is a statement or command made with a stated or implied corresponding dependent outcome. The condition, "For if you forgive others for their transgressions, [followed by the dependent outcome], your heavenly Father will also forgive you" (Matt 6:14). Note God will forgive if we meet his condition, and the clear implication is, if we do not meet his condition, he will not forgive us. Biblical conditionals highlight the vital truth that God's foreknowledge of everything does not mean everything is determined. Sometimes people confuse knowing with causing. God knows definite events because he determined them to happen apart from human influence, but he also knows indefinite events because he is essentially omniscient.[1]

By saying God is essentially omniscient, we mean omniscience is an essential property of who he is in the same way God is essentially omnipotent and omnipresent. Being essentially omniscient means that God innately knows all things he could have done, would do, and did do. God always knew what would take place based on what he created and the purpose of his creation. He does not look outside himself or look down or the halls of history to know this. Rather, he has always known himself and his intentions exhaustively, which includes the nature of his creation and the results of the actions of his creation.

He does not learn perceptively as we do; in fact, he does not learn at all, but, rather, he knows all because he is God. We often refer to his eternal knowledge of what will happen in time as foreknowledge. God always foreknew everything that would happen in time and space. Further, God cannot be wrong; he cannot hold a false belief about the future. Therefore, what he knows will happen will surely happen. This does not mean his eternal knowledge of future events causes all of them to happen, but it does assure these events will happen since God cannot hold a false belief. Therefore, God knowing something will happen does not require causality, but it does involve assurance since God cannot hold a false belief.

Everyone recognizes the Bible presents God and humans in a relationship, a state of affairs that was initiated by God. Scripture speaks about predestined definite events, conditional indefinite events, and mixed events. Mixed events refer to passages that contain both definite—predetermined—aspects and indefinite—affected by human choice—aspects.

Our choices and prayers make a difference in those areas where God has deemed human free will can influence an event. Prayerfully, this book will answer these nagging questions by demonstrating a harmonious relationship between the relational aspect of prayer and the power of prayer to change some things. All of which happens within God's sovereign rule of his creation in which he sovereignly weaves definite (determined) and indefinite (undetermined) events into the tapestry known as his will.

While this book focuses on the conditionals of Scripture (the prayer that changes outcomes), this is not to devalue prayer's power to change the individual or the fellowship of prayer. These are worthy of equal

1. See Authorial Glossary for definitions of definite events, indefinite events, and essentially omniscient.

consideration, but such suitable consideration of each would require an-other book. Additionally, praying in light of changing outcomes is not choosing this aspect of prayer over fellowship with God or being changed by prayer because a biblical understanding of conditionals actually increas-es and highlights those two components since a proper understanding of conditionals means that we walk in experiential communion with God in every area of life.

Regardless of the nature of the event, God is always sovereign over everything. He is equally sovereign over determined things as well as the undetermined things in which he determined to give man the privilege and responsibility of choice and prayer to influence outcomes and be affected by praying.

3

Understanding Who God Is

His Sovereignty and Omniscience

To UNDERSTAND THE PURPOSE, power, and effectiveness of prayer, we have to begin with a clear understanding of who God is because he is the one who designed prayer. He is the only one to whom we are to pray, and he is the only one who can answer prayer. There are two features of God that we need to consider for our study on prayer. First is God's sovereignty, which means God is over everything. He has supreme power and authority. He is jurisdictionally in charge of everything; therefore, he is in absolute charge of his universe. He is above everything in majesty, glory, authority, and power.[1] Second is God's omniscience, which means he knows everything. These two play an important role in understanding prayer and helping us keep a proper biblical perspective.

---

1. Calvinists use the term "sovereignty" to mean control so that God must micro-control every person, thought, and event through micro-determinism. He may use secondary causes, but he controls everything by predetermining every event apart from any efficacious acts and choices of humans. This definition fits Calvinism, but it is not the true meaning of the word, nor does it reflect the fullness of the Bible.

Understanding God's Sovereignty

"Have you not heard? Long ago I did it; From ancient times I planned it. Now I have brought it to pass, That you should turn fortified cities into ruinous heaps" (2 Kgs 19:25). God is declaring his sovereignty. God is telling them they will turn cities into ruinous heaps, but he planned it long ago. It is reminding them that everything is known by God and under his governance. This is his sovereignty. Isaiah says, "The Lord of hosts has sworn saying, 'Surely, just as I have intended so it has happened, and just as I have planned so it will stand'" (Isa 14:24). Because God is sovereign, there is no question whether what God has intended will happen or not. What we must determine is what God has intended in various areas of his creation and how did he intend for them to happen? Did God plan for the event you are facing to be predetermined, influenced by your choices and prayers, or one that is a mixture of all of them? That is at the heart of a true understanding of the meaning of prayer. Again, Isaiah proclaims, "O Lord, You are my God; I will exalt You, I will give thanks to Your name; For You have worked wonders, Plans formed long ago, with perfect faithfulness" (Isa 25:1).

Because God is who he is, he can say, "Declaring the end from the beginning, And from ancient times things which have not been done, Saying, 'My purpose will be established, And I will accomplish all My good pleasure'" (Isa 46:10). This Scripture tells us that whatever the will of God is, whatever his good pleasure is, he can say, "I will accomplish it." Because he is sovereign, we can fully trust that claim. His omnipotence also plays a role in this because he couldn't be sovereign if he were not all-powerful. He is all-powerful over creation, and there is nothing but God and creation, so it is a claim that only God can make.

"The counsel of the Lord stands forever, The plans of His heart from generation to generation" (Ps 33:11). Only one who is sovereign can say that. "The Lord looks from heaven; He sees all the sons of men; From His dwelling place He looks out On all the inhabitants of the earth, He who fashions the hearts of them all, He who understands all their works" (Ps 33:13–15). God fashioned the heart of man in creation, and he knew the desire to sin would rise up in the heart of man; he also always knew he would create a new heart in man in salvation. Regarding man's sinful heart, Jeremiah says, "The heart is more deceitful than all else And is desperately sick; Who can understand it" (Jer 17:9)? The next verse tells us only God can understand the heart of man, "I, the Lord, search the heart, I test the mind, Even to give to each man according to his ways, According to the results of his deeds" (Jer 17:10). "The Lord has made everything for its own purpose, Even the wicked for the day of evil" (Prov 16:4). "This passage is declaring that everything is according to God's plan; He is not surprised by the wicked man's choice to sin or continue to sin. Nor are the wicked or their wickedness out from under His plan. . . . God made those who are wicked—the wicked—but He did not make the wicked wicked."[2] To say it another way, even the wicked are not operating outside of his sovereign authority.

In John 19, we see an encounter between Jesus and Pilate. Pilate as governor, had a significant amount of authority. "Pilate says, 'You do not speak to me? Do You not know that I have authority to release You, and I have authority to crucify You?' Jesus answered, 'You would have no authority over Me, unless it had been given you from above; for this reason he who delivered Me to you has the greater sin'" (John 19:10–11). What is true of pharaohs, kings, Pilate, and other powerful people is also true of all people. God is the only one with innate authority. Everyone else has only delegated authority, delegated from God.

Some seem to think they can link select Scriptures to justify their claim that God must act as they have interpreted, make God somehow subject to our decisions, or suggest some area of reality beyond his authority and power. Prayerfully, we can immediately see how irreverent and untrue that is. How arrogant we are to think we can put the sovereign God in a box. Any view of reality that diminishes God's sovereign reign over his creation is flawed.

Understanding God's Omniscience

God's omniscience means he has *always* known everything. He does not look down the halls of time and learn what will happen by our choices. God innately knows everything. Isaiah said, "Who has directed the Spirit of the Lord, Or as His counselor has informed Him" (Isa 40:13)? Where are the teachers and dictionaries that have taught God what he knows? Of course,

---

2. Rogers, *Reflections*, 147. Calvinists often present this verse as teaching God created evil people, but that is not the meaning of the passage. Rather it emphasizes that God knew the people he created in holiness who would choose sin, and some would forever choose to remain in sin by rejecting his salvational love. For a full explanation of this passage, see *Reflections of a Disenchanted Calvinist*, chapter 20.

there are not any. "Behold, the former things have come to pass, Now I declare new things; Before they spring forth I proclaim them to you" (Isa 42:9).

"Who is like Me? Let him proclaim and declare it; Yes, let him recount it to Me in order, From the time that I established the ancient nation. And let them declare to them the things that are coming And the events that are going to take place. Do not tremble and do not be afraid; Have I not long since announced it to you and declared it? And you are My witnesses. Is there any God besides Me, Or is there any other Rock? I know of none" (Isa 44:7–8). "Therefore I declared them to you long ago, Before they took place I proclaimed them to you, So that you would not say, 'My idol has done them, And my graven image and my molten image have commanded them'" (Isa 48:5). Israel started worshiping idols they created and had God not predicted it, they would have attributed the work of God to their idols. But God declared it before they even had the idol.

Consider the words of God to Jeremiah the prophet, "Before I formed you in the womb I knew you, And before you were born I consecrated you; I have appointed you a prophet to the nations" (Jer 1:5). Think about the significance of this statement. God tells Jeremiah, I knew you before time. In my eternal mind, I always knew you because I always knew I would create you; I knew you before you existed in time, before time itself. Since God is omniscient, he cannot believe a false proposition. Whatever God believes is true. In eternity past, God knew Jeremiah innately and that he would live because he would create him in time.

Any view of reality that diminishes God eternally knowing everything that could, would, has, and will happen as an essential property of who he is, is flawed. As a result of who God is, when we are working through personal problems, we can be assured that God is the one we should pray to for help. He is sovereign, and he has always known about our situation. He is never surprised as we are. We may not understand the reasons for our situation, but we can rest in God's foreknowledge and sovereignty over our situation.

Often the will of God is presented as deterministic, and as such, the outcome of our prayers and even our choice to pray is determined. But that is an error. We know God works everything according to his will (Eph 1:11), and we are to pray according to his will (1 John 5:14). Accordingly, God's will is going to be done. That is not in question. The question is, what did God comprehend (include) in his will? Does God's will consist of only things he determined to happen, definite events that happen necessarily, or does it also include undetermined, indefinite events that happen certainly rather than necessarily; the latter refers to events that occur as a result of human choice.

Calvinists believe everything is determined, but Extensivists believe Scripture teaches that God included both determined and undetermined events. Consequently, the question is never whether God's will is going to be done, or are we to pray according to the will of God. But rather, what is included in the will of God. Once we know what God comprehends in his will, we will understand what it means to pray in the will of God. But we *cannot* know what it is to pray according to God's will without understanding what he included in his will.

Imagine you are in charge of cleaning a building. Your plan includes scheduling, equipment to be used, and how you plan to clean and keep the building cleaned. Then someone looks at the building and says, I thought you were going to clean this building. Why do I see three other people doing the work? To which you respond, they are in my plan to clean the building. My plan included having other people do the work for me. You created a plan and implemented it, but what confused the observer was his lack of full knowledge of your plan. He assumed you would be doing the work. His assumption was in error because he did not know that your plan would accomplish the goal in a very different way than he thought.

Similarly, when we talk about God's will, we need to understand what God comprehended in his will. I believe the Scripture presents God creating man with libertarian moral freedom. God's will includes events that are determined, and they will happen just as he has planned. His will also includes events that are the result of human choice. And while each individual is uncertain of what his future choice may actually be and how his freewill choices may impact an event, God has always known what every human choice would be and how every detail will work together. Neither facet detracts from God's sovereignty nor his omniscience as determinists contend, but rather it highlights them.

That God designed creation so that some outcomes are the result of human choices reemphasizes that God's permissive will is comprehended in his perfect will, and, therefore, what it means to pray in the will of God. His permissive will certainly includes the conditionals presented in Scripture, but it also seems to include conditionals for things outside of Scripture. The Scripture is God's objective will, which is for all people all the time. God also has a subjective will, which is always consistent with his objective will, but it is personal. That is to say, it is his will for a specific person at a specific time, which is not necessarily his will for anyone else. God's subjective will can include such things as whom to marry, how many children to have, where to live and work, or what part we play in the kingdom. Much of our prayers are in this area.

When someone seeks to present God's will as static, one-dimensional, or somehow meaning that everything is predetermined as consistent Calvinists do, they are importing their assumptions into the word "will" rather than letting the Scripture speak for itself. We call the Scripture the revealed will of God, and that is what it is. It is the revelation of his will. Therefore, his will comprehends everything revealed in Scripture. Scripture is the revelation of God's perfect and permissive will, in which we see some things as determined, some that are not, and some events that are a mixture of definite and certain aspects.

Everyone in orthodox Christianity agrees God knows the future. But we disagree about how God knows the future. I'm contrasting Calvinism, which relies solely on determinism, to Extensivism, which relies on God's essential omniscience. Calvinism believes God is omniscient and knows the future because he predetermined everything that is and will be.

Extensivism believes God is essentially omniscient, which means omniscience is an essential property of his deity, as are attributes like holiness, mercy, omnipresence, and omnipotence. Being essentially omniscient means that he can know determined events and undetermined events (contingencies), which happen as a result of human choice. Omniscience also means he cannot be wrong about anything.

Nothing happens that causes God to change his mind. In eternity past, God knew what we would do today. He does not learn by having looked into the future to see what we would do. He does not learn perceptively (learning or gaining insight), which is what we do. He knows everything innately because he is God. That's his nature. Whether God is directly causing something or permitting it, he has always known it eternally. There is no chronology in God's knowledge. He understands the sequence of events; for example, he always knew if he created the sun, heat and light would emanate from it, and if he created plants, they would grow from the light and heat. But he does not learn about the light or the effects of the light; he knows them innately because he eternally and exhaustively knows what creating the sun entails. Because he is essentially omniscient, he cannot fail to know the nature of the sun instinctively.

He eternally knew everything that he could do and would do, which includes everything associated with all he would create. He knows this not by looking outside himself but rather because he eternally and exhaustively knows himself and his intentions; that is a part of what it means to be essentially omniscient. Consequently, he always knew he would create the sun. And even before he created the sun, he knew there would be sunlight because he knew the essence of the sun. Similarly, God has always known what we would do because of who he is.

And in the Scripture, we see that he gave humans the ability to choose between accessible options. God always knew the essence of the beings he would create and call humans, which entailed they would have libertarian free will, and he would innately know every choice of all humans. That they could, in some situations, choose between accessible options was comprehended in his creation-redemption plan. With his eternal establishment of the range of options that people could choose from, he always knew what he associated with the choice and range. Scripture confirms this when God says he will bless this decision and curse this decision. Even when God unleashes his wrath, it is because people have made a willful choice to disobey him, which they did not have to make. As a result, we can and should pray for other people and trust God with the outcome, but we ought not to grow weary in prayer (Luke 18:1).

4

Understanding Who Man Is

What Does Free Will Mean?

IN CHAPTER 3, WE considered facets of God's nature as they relate to humans making choices and praying. Although we have already touched on the subject of man's free will, we will consider further the two views of man's free will and how the different perspectives relate to Scriptures that speak about choice, prayer, and man's responsibility. What we believe about God and how he created humans is vitally connected to our understanding of prayer, and our understanding of prayer is inextricably tied to our understanding of choice.

What do we mean when we say someone makes a choice, and more importantly, what does Scripture mean when it says a person chooses to believe or not believe, to pray or not pray? Although we sometimes think we all mean the same thing, we do not; the two views of free will are mutually exclusive.[1] According to Calvinism, God knows everything because he micro-determined everything, including the thoughts and actions of humans, by giving them compatible moral freedom. In Extensivism, God knows everything because he is essentially omniscient, and he gave man libertarian moral freedom—free will.

1. Some Calvinists do not use the term "free will" but only the term "moral freedom," although, I sometimes use them interchangeably. For a fuller understanding of these two views, see *Does God Love All or Some*, particularly chapter 7.

Compatibilism (compatible moral freedom) is the view that determinism and moral responsibility are compatible. Even though everything is determined, man is still considered to make a free choice for which he is responsible so long as it is according to his greatest desire. Even though his greatest desire is always determined by his past, and given his past, he could not have chosen differently than he did. When I use the term "determinism," I use it as defined in compatibilism.[2] In compatibilism, everything that has been, is, or will be is because God precisely determined it to be as it is.

For example, in prayer, a Calvinist may feel he chose to pray for someone rather than choosing not to pray for them. But if he is a consistent Calvinist, believing in determinism compatible style, he did not have a choice not to pray, even if he had an experiential sense he could. His choosing to pray was predetermined, including what he would say and what he would not say. As for the person who chose not to pray, that was predetermined by God as well. Accordingly, in true Calvinist theology, prayer does not change anything because everything is determined.

To veil the micro-determinism of compatibilism, Calvinists may say things like God uses secondary causes or man is the proximate (immediate) cause; both are true. However, true to determinism, from a biblical vantage point, means that God is the ultimate cause of everything. Everything is as he precisely determined it to be, and there can be no variation; this includes secondary causes.[3] Therefore, while man is the immediate cause, God, who gave him his past and nature from which his greatest desire originates, is the ultimate cause of everything, good and bad.

In compatibilism, God's permissive will is as determined as the rest of his will. Consequently, saying God permits something is not causally different than saying God determines something. Prayer that will change an outcome to be different is an illusion because everything is determined. Calvinists may say it is a part of the process, but it is still true that the choice to pray and words prayed are as determined as is the unalterable object of that prayer.

Millard Erickson, a moderate Calvinist, referring to the exhaustive and comprehensive nature of God's determinative plan, says, "God rendered it

2. As opposed to hard or raw determinism, which says man is not morally responsible since everything is determined.

3. God's micro-determinism includes secondary causes and every cause, whether we are talking about remoter causes such as tertiary, quaternary, quinary, senary, septenary, octonary, nonary, or denary.

certain that at that one particular point I would freely move my finger to the right."[4] In contrasting Calvinism and Arminianism, Erickson says, "Calvinists believe that . . . *human decisions and actions are a consequence* . . . God in his plan has chosen that some shall believe and thus receive the offer of eternal life. *He foreknows what will happen because he has decided what is to happen. This is true with respect to all other human decisions and actions as well . . . God's decision has rendered it certain that every individual will act in a particular way*"[5] (italics added). Therefore, all human decisions and actions are a consequence of God's determinative will. That being true, it is accurate to say God has rendered not only *certain* but *necessary* "that every individual will act in a particular way." Actions and events happen necessarily since any modification would break the chain of determinative antecedents that lead back to God, who is the ultimate cause.

Calvinist Wayne Grudem provides an example of Calvinists delicately speaking about the deterministic nature of prayer so that it easy to miss. The words in brackets are mine for clarification. He says, "God has also ordained [predetermined] that prayer is a very significant means of bringing about results in the world. [Although he does not say it, understand prayer is a predetermined means that cannot change a predetermined outcome.] When we earnestly intercede for a specific person or situation, we will often find that God had ordained [predetermined] that our prayer would be a means he would use to bring about the changes in the world. [A predetermined means God predetermined to use to bring about his predetermined plan]"[6] Grudem then cites two verses that do not support his determined use of prayer because they are conditionals, Jas 4:2 and John 16:24, which teach the very opposite of determinism. Notice in Grudem's words, there is no concept of conditionals because everything is determined. Any sense that Calvinists have a choice to pray or not pray or can change an outcome is an illusion.

Libertarian free will says determinism and moral responsibility are not compatible. A person is considered to make a free choice so long as he could have chosen differently in the moral moment of decision, given the same past. He can choose to act or refrain.[7] His past can influence his

4. Erickson, *Christian Theology*, 1:358.

5. Erickson, *Christian Theology*, 1:326.

6. Grudem, *Systematic Theology*, 334.

7. Technically, it is more precise to say that a person, given the same past, could have chosen differently than he did in some situations since libertarian freedom does not

choice, but it is not determinative or causal. The person objectively deliberates because he is truly deciding between various available options, and his decision can change the course of his future. The future will be different if he chooses differently, which choice is in his power at the moment of decision.

Libertarian freedom does not mean that a person can do anything. It does not mean that *every* choice must be undetermined, but only that *some* are. Having one's libertarian choice overridden does not eliminate a person's libertarian free will; it only means he is not responsible for that particular decision. A different range of options for different people does not change the fact of libertarian free will, only what options are available. For example, people in different cities, states, or countries may have options that others do not, but all can have libertarian free will; even as a person ages, his options may change, but his possession of libertarian free will does not. I still have free will, but I cannot choose to run as fast as I did when I was sixteen.

In prayer, this means a person can choose to pray or not to pray. If you choose to pray in response to conditionals God has given, you receive what you would not have received if you had not asked. For example, "But if any of you lacks wisdom, let him ask of God, who gives to all generously and without reproach, and it will be given to him" (Jas 1:5). God promises to give wisdom if you meet the condition of asking. Given libertarian freedom and conditionals, prayer can change some things so that they, and sometimes even you, will be different than if you had not prayed, and you could have chosen not to pray. In this conditional, the person who prayed for wisdom regarding a situation would have God's wisdom that he would not have if he chose not to pray.

In libertarianism, God's permissive will refers to God permitting us to make some choices that are not his desire for us, and they are, therefore, not his best for us. One example is allowing a person to reject trusting Christ in salvation, or even when a Christian chooses to disobey, not grow spiritually, or not pray. Within the limits of his permissive will, God will let us choose our own way instead of his desired will for us. From the libertarian point of view, when you pray about your child, for example, God can use your prayer to affect what happens to your child. And if you do not pray for your child, the result you desire may not happen because there is a substantive

---

entail that God has not determined some things.

and essential relationship between the prayer and the outcome, which God has designed in his will.

When we look at some of the verses on prayer, it seems like God has left various options open. Accordingly, it seems like if we pray, God will fulfill his conditional promises, and if we do not pray, God will withhold his conditioned promises. Scripture says, if you believe, you will be saved, and if you do not believe, you will not be saved (John 3:18). From a clear, objective reading, this appears to be a real choice between accessible options that can result in different consequences. The outcomes are conditional, which is only consistent with a libertarian free will perspective.[8]

---

8. When we show some of the conditionals in Scripture, Calvinists are prone to say that we are not showing all the verses that teach determinism, which is true. Their point is that if we do not show all of them in our study, we are skewing the teaching of Scripture. My response is, first, we will look at verses wherein God determined the outcome. We readily acknowledge God determines some outcomes, but we also acknowledge that he has determined some outcomes to be the result of human influence. Second, we need not look at every verse that indicates outcomes are determined or undetermined because, while libertarian freedom comprehends both, compatibilism does not. If only one verse or passage can be found in the Bible that teaches a choice between accessible options in which the person can choose or not choose in the moral moment of decision with the same past with corresponding consequences, compatibilism fails as a biblically viable explanation of mankind's moral freedom.

5

Biblical Examples of People Choosing
to Serve or Not Serve God

THIS CHAPTER HIGHLIGHTS BIBLICAL examples of people making choices. The question you must ask yourself is do these instances *merely look like* the individuals are exercising free will because God had already determined everything to happen as it did? That is, do they reflect compatibilism? Or, do they reflect people with free will *who chose between accessible options*, and whatever they did choose, they could have chosen differently? That is, do they reflect libertarian free will? I am convinced that reading the Scripture as it is makes it clear from beginning to end that people are accountable to God for their choices because they could have chosen differently in most circumstances.

A biblical understanding of what it means to make a choice is essential to understanding prayer, particularly in the area of conditionals (Prov 28:13–14). The question of choice must be answered to fully grasp the significance of praying, God's promises in response to prayers, and the potential loss of God's blessing due to our lack of praying.

Genesis 2–3

Let us look at Adam and Eve in Genesis and focus on the tree of the knowledge of good and evil (Gen 2:17) and their choice to distrust God (Gen 3:1–6). I know this is a familiar story. But the question is, does a normal and unstrained reading of Genesis present Adam and Eve making a predetermined free choice or a choice in which they could have and should have chosen differently?

First, we need to note the prohibition given to Adam in chapter 2. "Then the Lord God took the man and put him into the Garden of Eden to cultivate it and keep it. The Lord God commanded the man, saying, 'From any tree of the garden you may eat freely; but from the tree of the knowledge of good and evil you shall not eat, for in the day that you eat from it you will surely die'" (Gen 2:15–17). Does that appear to be describing an event in which God gave Adam a command not to eat when he had already predetermined that Adam could only choose to eat of the tree? Or was the command not to eat something Adam could genuinely choose to do or not do?

Genesis 3 describes the temptation and the fall.

> Now the serpent was more crafty than any beast of the field which the Lord God had made. And he said to the woman, "Indeed, has God said, 'You shall not eat from any tree of the garden?'" The woman said to the serpent, "From the fruit of the trees of the garden we may eat; but from the fruit of the tree which is in the middle of the garden, God has said, 'You shall not eat from it or touch it, or you will die.'" The serpent said to the woman, "You surely will not die! For God knows that in the day you eat from it your eyes will be opened, and you will be like God, knowing good and evil." When the woman saw that the tree was good for food, and that it was a delight to the eyes, and that the tree was desirable to make one wise, she took from its fruit and ate; and she gave also to her husband with her, and he ate. (Gen 3:1–6)

We first see Eve deliberating about what the serpent said and framing a response based on her considerations. Also, the temptations are very specific. There are dialogue and discussion about whom to believe, God, or herself and the serpent. Then, after the fall we find these words.

> They heard the sound of the Lord God walking in the garden in the cool of the day, and the man and his wife hid themselves from the presence of the Lord God among the trees of the garden. Then the Lord God called to the man, and said to him, "Where are you?" He said, "I heard the sound of You in the garden, and I was afraid because I was naked; so I hid myself." And He said, "Who told you that you were naked? Have you eaten from the tree of which I commanded you not to eat?" (Gen 3:8–11)

We have to know that if God commanded them not to eat, and a person believes in a deterministic view, then he has to believe that along with the command not to eat, God gave them a history that would produce their greatest desire, which necessitated that they would freely eat. Therefore, this viewpoint has God punishing them for doing the very thing he predetermined them to do, which also brings up the issue of ultimate responsibility for sin. Or do you believe God's depiction of the event is more reflective of man having the free will to either obey or not obey God's command not to eat, and that God truly desired they not eat, as demonstrated by his command not to eat and the sufficient provision he had given in the garden?

Further along in the narrative, we find God pronouncing judgment on the serpent, "The Lord God said to the serpent, 'Because you have done this, cursed are you more than all cattle, and more than every beast of the field; on your belly you will go, and dust you will eat all the days of your life'" (Gen 3:14). Notice the cause and effect: because you did this, I curse you. It gives every indication that if he had not done this, God would not have judged him for tempting Eve. The judgment was based on his choice.

In verse 16, God doesn't explicitly say to Eve because you have done this, but it seems implied because the woman is placed between the man and Satan. "To the woman He said, 'I will greatly multiply your pain in childbirth, in pain you will bring forth children; yet your desire will be for your husband, and he will rule over you'" (Gen 3:16). God told her he would take the most incredible blessing he gave her, which is procreation, something that should have been filled with only joy and make it plagued by pain, disappointment, and death. As the mother of all living, her sin jeopardized the whole human race. Every indication is that the judgment on her was because she trusted the serpent over God.

"Then to Adam He said, 'Because you have listened to the voice of your wife, and have eaten from the tree about which I commanded you, saying, 'You shall not eat from it'; cursed is the ground because of you; in toil you will eat of it all the days of your life'" (Gen 3:17). Notice the causal relationship again; the condition, "because you listened to the voice of your wife," and the consequence, "cursed." The clear implication is that he didn't have to follow Eve, and he should not have. Without a prior commitment to determinism, I do not believe you can understand it to mean that Adam should not have listened to Eve and that he could not have chosen not to listen. God tells Adam the judgment is because he did not obey the command not to eat. In verse 23, God banishes them from the garden.

If you read that passage without any theological prejudice or a preconceived ideological destination in mind, it is obvious the text is not written in a way to evidence that Adam and Eve were judged for wrongs they were predetermined to commit. If compatibilism is true, as Calvinism asserts, God did ultimately desire and determine them to sin.

And if he desired that sin, then he desires all sin: every murder, every robbery, every child abuse, and every other breach of holiness, which is undeniable since he predetermined every action and thought of every human being. And being God, he could have given them a different past that, according to compatibilism, would have determined that Adam and Eve would have chosen not to sin. The only reason he did not is that it did not please him to do so (Eph 1:11). To avoid this reality, Calvinists respond, "It is an inscrutable mystery." While they may exonerate God from being the proximate cause (the person acting or closest to the sin), given compatibilism, that does not acquit him from being the ultimate cause of sin. Unfortunately for Calvinists, that is the inescapable nature of compatibilism.

The only way of not implicating God as ultimately responsible for sin is by recognizing that God created Adam and Eve and their progeny with libertarian freedom. That means they had the ability to eat or not eat, to love God or not love him, just as God freely chose to love them. In this view, he truly desired Adam and Eve to obey his command because he loves his creation and always desires holiness and righteousness. And even while he desires that mankind not sin, he comprehended man's misuse of his freedom and made provision for that in his coextensive creation-redemption plan. Free will is a good gift from God, whereas the sin of man is the misuse of God's good gift. These are our only two choices. You can't mix libertarian and compatibilist views. They are mutually exclusive.[1]

That is why it is essential to know and understand the nature of God and man because this deeply affects why we pray, what prayer is all about, and what we should expect from our prayers, which are intertwined with

---

1. Do not be sidetracked by answers that say Adam could have refrained intellectually, but not morally. The question is not whether part of the person could have resisted eating; instead, it is could the person Adam or the person Eve have refrained from sinning in the moral moment of decision in the garden? The answer, according to compatibilism, is NO! Compatibilism means God created them so they could not follow his command, not merely that they would not. The portrait painted by compatibilism is a strikingly different picture of a different God and different man than is portrayed in Scripture. I would add to this, a person may argue determinism and compatibilism philosophically, but no one can live a consistently determined life; at least, I have never heard of or seen anyone that does.

our motivation to pray. If man was determined to freely choose to sin, then it is impossible to glean any possibility of prayer ever affecting a different outcome than is predetermined to happen, despite biblical promises that it will. Prayers for different outcomes for our children, the spread of the gospel, and our spiritual lives is a cruel illusion. But, as we will see, the biblical teaching about prayer is the very opposite of dark determinism.

Joshua 24

The previous passage, in part, dealt with the pre-fall era. But what about choosing whether or not to serve God in the post-fall era? Because prayer is a choice, sin could have made it impossible to choose to follow God, believe in Christ, follow Christ, or even whether to pray or not after we are saved. Joshua chapter 24 details a challenge put forth by Joshua to Israel. The challenge is between God and idolatry. Before he gives the challenge to forsake idolatry and serve God, he reminds them of what God had done for them. Chapter 24 is a summary of what God had done for Israel. Here are a few highlights:

> Verse 3: "Then I took your father Abraham . . . and led him through all the land of Canaan, and multiplied his descendants and gave him Isaac." Verse 4: "To Isaac I gave Jacob and Esau." Verse 5: "Then I sent Moses and Aaron, and I plagued Egypt." Verse 6: "I brought your fathers out of Egypt." Verse 8: "Then I brought you into the land of the Amorites . . . and I gave them into your hands." Verses 12–13: "Then I sent the hornet before you and it drove out the two kings of the Amorites from before you, but not by your sword or your bow. I gave you a land on which you had not labored, and cities which you had not built, and you have lived in them; you are eating of vineyards and olive groves which you did not plant."

Then comes God's challenge to Israel through Joshua. Verse 14 says, "Now, therefore, fear the Lord and serve Him in sincerity and truth; and put away the gods which your fathers served beyond the River and in Egypt, and serve the Lord." That is the choice before the Israelites. Choose to abandon idolatry and serve God, or they can, despite all that God has done for them, stay in their sinful idolatry. It is all about choosing. This would make no sense if they were determined by God to be in idolatry in the first place. And if they were determined to serve him, they could not choose to remain in idolatry. It does not seem that anyone could deduce such a state of affairs from the scriptural language. It only makes sense as a conditional, where the Jews are called to choose between accessible options. They can choose to remain in idolatry or choose to obey God and follow him; from a compatible perspective, it seems to make God either incapable of speaking clearly about reality as it truly is or intentionally misleading his people about reality.

Verse 15 goes on to say, "If it is disagreeable in your sight to serve the Lord, choose for yourselves today whom you will serve: whether the gods which your fathers served which were beyond the River, or the gods of the Amorites in whose land you are living; but as for me and my house, we will serve the Lord." The first question is, how could it possibly be disagreeable if God has determined everything? The "if" introduces a conditional, not something predestined. In the previous challenge, he gave two options, but now he expands the options to three. There is deliberation when faced with an either-or decision, but even more so when there are multiple options, each with benefits and cost. We often find ourselves in similar situations. We have multiple options with their own benefits and cost. Joshua, who has the same choice, states that he has chosen to reject pagan idols beyond the river and Amorite gods and serve God. We see this when people choose to serve God and others choose not to serve him. This passage gives every appearance that this is a clear choice between accessible options. There is not even a hint of determinism in this event; it is only there if unwarrantedly imported.

The people's response to Joshua comes from deliberating, not giving a predetermined response. Verse 16: "The people answered and said, 'Far be it from us that we should forsake the Lord to serve other gods.'" The people understood the choices, and they were clear about what they were not going to do. Verse 17: "For the Lord our God is He who brought us and our fathers up out of the land of Egypt, from the house of bondage, and who did these great signs in our sight and preserved us through all the way in which we went and among all the peoples through whose midst we passed." Here we see the people deliberating by remembering what Joshua said and what God did, and they reflect on their idolatrous state in comparison with following God. They seem to know this is a choice they need to make, and there will be consequences based on what they choose. Just as we see throughout Scripture and in our own lives, life is about the choices we make. Choices, including the choice to pray or not pray, change some things so that new possibilities are accessible that would not be so had we chosen differently.

Verse 18: "The Lord drove out from before us all the peoples, even the Amorites who lived in the land. We also will serve the Lord, for He is our God." That's their choice. But notice Joshua gave them a choice between serving and not serving. There is every indication that they could have chosen not to serve. We do the same thing. We deliberate and think through choices put before us, and then we choose. We may make the wrong choice. We may make a different choice than we would have had we chosen later. We may regret our choice or be happy about our choice, but we choose between real accessible options. And, as here, we see the call of God for people to choose between sin and serving him, neither being the result of a determined outcome.

Joshua then detects some insincerity. Verses 19–20: "Then Joshua said to the people, 'You will not be able to serve the Lord, for He is a holy God. He is a jealous God; He will not forgive your transgression or your sins. If you forsake the Lord and serve foreign gods, then He will turn and do you harm and consume you after He has done good to you.'" Here again, is a causal relationship between the choices people make and judgment. God will not forgive "if" they forsake him after committing to serve him. These are all conditional statements that only make sense in a world of libertarian free will.

So, the people listened to Joshua and deliberated and chose. Verses 21–22: "The people said to Joshua, 'No, but we will serve the Lord.' Joshua said to the people, 'You are witnesses against yourselves that you have chosen for yourselves the Lord, to serve Him.' And they said, 'We are witnesses.'" They considered what was said, the options before them, and made a choice. And they were the witnesses testifying that they had truly chosen to reject idols and follow God.

Verse 23: "Now therefore, put away the foreign gods which are in your midst, and incline your hearts to the Lord, the God of Israel." Why does Joshua say, therefore? It is based on their choice to abandon the idols and serve God that Joshua told them to incline their hearts to God. I believe in the total depravity of man, and these are fallen people.[2] Because of the fall, humans cannot initiate a spiritually restorative move toward God apart

---

2. By total depravity of man, I mean sin affected every part of man, and, therefore, I reject partial depravity. Further, I do not accept Calvinism's definition of total depravity, which includes man being endowed with compatible moral freedom.

from the grace of God. God works in grace, so the effects of the fall do not keep us from making spiritually restorative choices. Notice that they were called to choose God, and now they are also to incline their hearts to God. They are to choose to grow more, learn, and live as God commands. This is similar to learning God's word or discipling someone; we are trying to incline hearts toward God. The same is true for our children. We do not want them just to learn things from the Bible; we want to teach and lead them in such a way to encourage them to incline their hearts toward God. It seems obvious that we are not determined, or without sufficient grace in the post-fall era, if we can choose whether or not to incline our heart toward God.

Verse 24: "The people said to Joshua, 'We will serve the Lord our God, and we will obey His voice.'" We will do this. They are essentially saying that we know our fathers sinned, and we do not want to make the same bad choices. So, based on the knowledge we have and the options before us, we choose to follow and serve God. We will obey his voice.

> Verses 25–27: So Joshua made a covenant with the people that day, and made for them a statute and an ordinance in Shechem. And Joshua wrote these words in the book of the law of God; and he took a large stone and set it up there under the oak that was by the sanctuary of the Lord. Joshua said to all the people, "Behold, this stone shall be for a witness against us, for it has heard all the words of the Lord which He spoke to us; thus it shall be for a witness against you, so that you do not deny your God."

From these verses, we see that even after they chose to follow God, another choice follows; the choice to covenant together to be faithful to their decision to follow God. The focus is their solemn commitment to serve Jehovah, which would entail keeping the law. The stone served as a legal reminder of the covenant that all of them chose and agreed to enter into with God. The stone hearing is a metaphor that is a witness to what God had said to them and his faithfulness. The stone reminded them of their willing covenant with God, much like a picture can remind us of an occasion. The stone served as a visual aid for them to be faithful to their choice to forsake idolatry, follow Jehovah, and do so by covenant. As humans, we must not only choose to obey God, but we must continue to choose to follow God, which is the life of repeatedly choosing God over every idol that is a wannabe god. If they were determined to follow God, any reminder or encouragement to do so is pointless.

What we see in this passage is that Joshua laid out the case of the Lord, which included the example of their fathers choosing sin and idolatry, God's displeasure with them, and a clear call for these Israelites to reject the path of their fathers, recognize God's goodness, and choose to obey God's commands. Then there is the covenant and the stone, legal witnesses of each other, as well as their decision to follow God. The need for the stone and the covenant, witnesses of our words, remind us there is always a choice to deny God even after a serious commitment to be faithful to him. To read this narrative through the lens of compatibilism, which precludes the ability to choose differently in the moral moment of decision, makes the whole encounter unintelligible and meaningless. That is why a determinist would probably teach it in a strikingly similar way to the way I have. The only problem is such would be inconsistent with Calvinism's determinism.

I remember preaching in a country church when I was a new pastor. When I gave the invitation, a man came down the aisle in a wheelchair and told me that God had called him to preach. He said that call had been 30 years earlier. He said he chose not to answer that call of God. Then he said he had known every day of his life that was why he has been in a wheelchair all these years. He said, "I am under the discipline of the Lord." Our choices have consequences!

We, like the Israelites, are required to choose and choose often. We counsel people to choose to follow God. We tell them God is good; trust him. And if you don't, there are consequences. But if there is no real choice, none of that makes sense. If everything is determined as Calvinism teaches, then it is at best nonsense and at worst an evil deception. If Calvinism is correct, we are all determined to choose what we choose and could not choose differently in the moral moment of decision; therefore, your suffering and evil, as is another person's good and blessing, are what God precisely determined for both of you. Why pray, obey God, and teach our children to do the same?

The idea of reward or punishment is best understood if there is a choice to have done otherwise. We extol or reward heroes because they chose to do something heroic instead of acting cowardly or doing nothing. We punish those who choose to do corrupt things because they could have chosen not to act corruptly. We see this in the prayers of Jeremiah. "Who shows lovingkindness to thousands, but repays the iniquity of fathers into the bosom of their children after them, O great and mighty God. The Lord of hosts is His name" (Jer 32:18). Notice that God shows lovingkindness to thousands, but when you commit iniquity, he punishes, and other generations can suffer for the sins of their fathers.

Jeremiah 32

The choice to disobey God always results in judgment and loss. Here we are provided with another example of people making real choices between accessible options with very different consequences. Jeremiah, speaking of God, says, "Great in counsel and mighty in deed, whose eyes are open to all the ways of the sons of men, giving to everyone according to his ways and according to the fruit of his deeds" (Jer 32:19). God knows what he predetermined to happen. But he also knows what he permits man to choose to do so that he knows all the ways of man simply because he is essentially omniscient. Because he is just, he gives to man according to his ways and deeds. God's reward is just because man could have chosen evil when he chose good and, he could have chosen good when he chose evil. If one man were determined to choose only evil and the other only good, rewards would be meaningless. But with actual choices that could be different, rewards are intrinsically connected to man's choices.

Jeremiah then says, "They came in and took possession of it, but they did not obey Your voice or walk in Your law; they have done nothing of all that You commanded them to do; therefore You have made all this calamity come upon them" (Jer 32:23). This only makes sense if the Israelites had libertarian free will, which the passage reflects. God commanded, but they did not obey when the text makes it clear that he believed they could have and should have. You say, how do I know they had a choice to obey? It was because of God's response to their disobedience when Jeremiah said, "Therefore You have made all this calamity come upon them."

A simple reading of the passage tells us they were put in the land, shown lovingkindness, and blessed by God. Despite that, they didn't obey God, and they didn't walk in his law. Why did the calamity come on them? Were they predetermined to disobey, and God wanted to cause them pain? Or did God give them the freedom to experience his blessings, but they chose to disobey? And they chose to disobey even though God had blessed, shown lovingkindness, gave the land, and conquered their enemies. There is a penalty when there is sin, and God brought calamity on them because of their choice to sin.

"Therefore thus says the Lord, 'Behold, I am about to give this city into the hand of the Chaldeans and into the hand of Nebuchadnezzar king of Babylon, and he will take it. The Chaldeans who are fighting against this city will enter and set this city on fire and burn it, with the houses where people have offered incense to Baal on their roofs and poured out drink offerings to other gods to provoke Me to anger'" (Jer 32:28–29). The people had all the blessings of God, yet, they practiced paganism, worshiped Baal, kept none of God's commands, and provoked God to anger.

This passage needs no explanation if the people had libertarian free will wherein they could have and should have chosen to obey. But if they were determined, God would not be genuinely provoked to anger because he would have predetermined their sinful rebellion. To be provoked at their actions that he predetermined seems to imply he was provoked with himself. Clearly, there was a choice, and God is displeased by their choice. It is not God's desire that they worship other gods. Was it God's plan to permit them that choice? Yes! Or they would not have had the choice because God is sovereign. But it is not his desire that they sin. He is a righteous God, and he will judge sin. He permits their choice to sin, as he did Adam and Eve, but he did not desire it.

"'Indeed the sons of Israel and the sons of Judah have been doing only evil in My sight from their youth; for the sons of Israel have been only provoking Me to anger by the work of their hands,' declares the Lord" (Jer 32:30). The passage doesn't make sense if you believe their thoughts and actions were predetermined. But it makes perfect sense if a holy God blesses people, and they use their hands and minds and wills to do evil. And while God permitted it, he does not desire it, and it provokes him to anger.

"Because of all the evil of the sons of Israel and the sons of Judah which they have done to provoke Me to anger—they, their kings, their leaders, their priests, their prophets, the men of Judah and the inhabitants of Jerusalem. They have turned their back to Me and not their face; though I taught them, teaching again and again, they would not listen and receive instruction" (Jer 32:32–33). The options before the people were to either turn their back on God or turn their face to God. It is clear God was teaching them to act righteously, but "they would not listen and receive instruction," which is evidenced by the fact they did evil.

6

Biblical Examples of God Determining Events without Human Influence

PRAYER IS A CHOICE. We are commanded to pray, expected to pray, and blessed when we do pray, but we are not forced to pray; it is a choice. Understanding prayer, particularly the conditional nature of some prayers, requires a clear understanding of how God interacts with those created in his image. God has determined that some things are, by their very nature, unaffected by human choice or prayer. At other times, he desires to permit human choice to affect outcomes, and in other events, God determines some part while human choice influences some part. The same is true with prayer because prayer is a significantly relational experience in which we find some things determined by God and others that he designed to be influenced by our prayers. The result is some outcomes are changeable by prayer, and some are not. In this chapter, we will look at biblical examples of events that are determined.[1]

Matthew 20:20–23

This passage is an interesting example.

> Then the mother of the sons of Zebedee came to Jesus with her sons, bowing down and making a request of Him. And He said to her, "What do you wish?" She said to Him, "Command that in

1. Even some of the examples given as determined in this chapter or affected by choice in the previous chapter may actually be a mixture of both.

Your kingdom these two sons of mine may sit one on Your right and one on Your left." But Jesus answered, "You do not know what you are asking. Are you able to drink the cup that I am about to drink?" They said to Him, "We are able." He said to them, "My cup you shall drink; but to sit on My right and on My left, this is not Mine to give, but it is for those for whom it has been prepared by My Father." (Matt 20:20–23)

The mother rightly recognizes Jesus as the King of the coming kingdom. But she errs in thinking that he makes every decision regarding the kingdom, and those decisions can be humanly influenced. Jesus replies that the Father has prepared (predetermined) who sits in these places of honor; that is a settled issue. As a result, no matter what you ask, who asks, what you pray, or what you do, this particular issue has been predetermined by God the Father and not only is unalterable, it cannot be known until the Father reveals it.

It might be that the sons put their mother up to this, which demonstrates a lack of humility if they did. Asking such a question may have been presumptuous even if Jesus did have the power. But we can also see that as a mother, she understandably wanted the best for her sons. If we are going to ask something of God, why ask the worst or something mediocre? As parents, we may need to check our impertinence and overly ambitious requests of God by closing our requests with "Your will be done." But desiring the best for our child is not inherently sinful. While it is natural to desire good things for our loved ones, we do not know what God has predetermined and what can be altered by choice or prayer. As a result, we must realize that God may not answer some of our prayer requests, and knowing his goodness and that he is sovereign, we should be content with his answers (1 Tim 6:6).

Matthew 24:22

This has to do with the length of the tribulation period. "Unless those days had been cut short, no life would have been saved; but for the sake of the elect those days will be cut short" (Matt 24:22). Those seven years are going to be so horrible that if they continued, soaked in the sinfulness of man, no lives would be saved. If man were able to run his full sinful course unbridled, it would thwart the plan of God. But that will not happen. God will intervene and override man's freedom to keep his plan moving forward.

Notice God decides to cut it short. There is no human involvement in the decision or the timing. It is not a conditional statement.

Matthew 24:36

Christ speaks of his second coming. "But of that day and hour no one knows, not even the angels of heaven, nor the Son, but the Father alone" (Matt 24:36). The time of Christ's coming is known only by the Father. That is something God alone determined, predestined, and did not consider human involvement in any sense. Not only that, he is not going to reveal the appointed time regardless of man's attempts to figure it out.

In application, Matthew reminds us that when disaster strikes or our lives fall apart, God is not absent. He is actively involved. Although we pray and pray, thinking we cannot go on, God always provides a way out, sometimes providing sunshine at just the right time. The second coming example reminds us that although times can become chaotic, dark, and lonely, and we do not know how we will survive, we can look up because Christ will return and make all things new.

Acts 1:6

In Acts chapter 1, the disciples kept asking Jesus when he was going to restore the kingdom to Israel (Acts 1:6). The word *ask* is in the present tense in the original, which signifies a continuous or repetitive action. "He said to them, 'It is not for you to know times or epochs which the Father has fixed by His own authority'" (Acts 1:7). They were anxious for Christ to inaugurate the promised Messianic reign on the throne of David, but Jesus said it is not for them to know the time or the chronology of when the kingdom would be established. Essentially, he, albeit quite gently, tells them it is none of their business because God has fixed the time, and nothing is going to change it. The word fixed in the original is *tithemi*, and it means "times which the Father has caused to be on his own authority" or "established on his own authority."[2] The event and its time of initiation have been determined by God alone. Not only did man not play a part in the timing, but he also is not even allowed to know the time. Practically speaking, this provides a great principle to apply. In our personal lives and families, there

2. Louw and Nida, *Greek-English Lexicon*, 149.

can be situations we do not influence because God has determined or permitted things to happen. The question then is, can we be content to trust him with that (Phil 4:11)? Another application may be something we have prayed about, and it seems like God says no, when he may be saying wait. The truth was God would inaugurate his kingdom. That it was not happening at that moment is no indication that it is not going to happen. Only God knows everything that he has determined and not determined as well as the timing. He is worthy of our trust.

Acts 21:24

Here, we find a prediction about the fall of Jerusalem, but it's broader than that. It says, "And they will fall by the edge of the sword, and will be led captive into all the nations; and Jerusalem will be trampled underfoot by the Gentiles until the times of the Gentiles are fulfilled" (Acts 21:24). I believe the times of the gentiles refers to the time in which gentile nations exercise dominion over Israel. This period began when Jerusalem fell to Babylon in 586 BC, and it extends to the end of the Tribulation when Christ sets up his kingdom. The time of the gentiles, like the time of the Messianic kingdom, has been set by God, and it will be fulfilled by God. It was not established, nor can it be changed by human actions, even prayer. It is a definite, determined event.

An application is that there are some things we would not want alterable by human involvement. Our security rests in knowing God will accomplish his purpose, which requires that humans cannot change some things. At times we pray for God to change an event or outcome. But as we mature in our faith, we can look back and see that request was not best. In a sense, we are often like a small child who thinks his request is for his good, but we know it is not. Accordingly, we thank God for those things he has determined unalterable, and we rest in "Your will be done."

Romans 11:25

In the book of Romans, Jews are described in the privileged position as the covenant people. But in the New Testament era, God has temporarily cut off the Jews, nationally speaking, and is working among the gentile nations. "For I do not want you, brethren, to be uninformed of this mystery—so that you will not be wise in your own estimation—that a partial hardening has happened to Israel until the fullness of the Gentiles has come in" (Rom 11:25). A mystery in the Bible refers to something that has not been revealed until now. God is primarily talking about his salvation plan. And this present time when he is working predominately among the gentile nations does not go on forever. It may be unknown to us, but God has fixed the time of the end.

Maybe the end is set according to when a certain number of people are saved, perhaps it is a specific number of days, or maybe it is a mixture of those. Whatever it is, God has determined he will fulfill his plan. But notice there is no human involvement in establishing "the fullness of the Gentiles." God does not indicate that it can be altered by human choice or prayer. It is not conditional.

In application, we can take great comfort that God established this parameter and will one day remove the hardening of Israel as a nation and fulfill every relevant promise that is associated with that removal. We can always trust there is only one who knows all the facts, who is truly good, and who will complete his plan glorifying himself and blessing his people. When God determines something, unlike humans and Satan, no one can alter it. Therefore, we are secure in him and because of him, regardless of the situation. Another possible applicatory thought is that God may have a season set for a period in our lives. Maybe that involves discipline or hardship, but just because something is happening now does not mean it has no end.

1 Corinthians 2:6–8

Paul says, "Yet we do speak wisdom among those who are mature; a wisdom, however, not of this age nor of the rulers of this age, who are passing away; but we speak God's wisdom in a mystery, the hidden wisdom which God predestined before the ages to our glory; the wisdom which none of the rulers of this age has understood; for if they had understood it they would not have crucified the Lord of glory" (1 Cor 2:6–8). The wisdom of which Paul speaks is the knowledge of redemption, particularly the death, burial, and resurrection of Christ. Man's study, research, or mental acuity cannot discover redemption because God sovereignly predetermined that it could only be known by revelation.

These verses declare that if man had been able to figure out that Jesus was God incarnate, he would not have crucified him. But God decided in his eternal plan that the wisdom of salvation would be revealed, not learned as one learns science or philosophy. We see this truth even today. Salvation is not dependent or understood based on a certain level of intelligence or education but is only available by God's grace and revelation. Humans can do phenomenally astonishing and significant things, yet they cannot figure out salvation on their own because it is a wisdom that God determined to disclose by revelation.[3]

The application is clear. God's choice to make salvation known by revelation and the power of the gospel is so that anyone can know and receive God's redemptive offer. In like manner, we can rest assured that God always desires the best for people because he desires and provisioned their eternal salvation. This desire of God is neither prompted by man's worth nor acquired by man's merit but is available because of the mercy, grace, and love of God (John 3:16). That is true of all the blessings of God in our lives.

These are just a few examples of God predetermining some things so that human involvement, even requests and prayers by his children, cannot affect his determined outcome. Examples of God's predetermination are important for our spiritual life. But it is also important not to be troubled when a Calvinist shows you Scriptures that declare or demonstrate God predestining events. Instead, say, well, of course, he has. Since Calvinism requires everything to be determined, they are prone to emphasize the determinative aspect of God's plan beyond what is biblically justifiable.

Remember that just because some things are predetermined does not mean all things are predetermined. All we have to find is one passage in the Scripture, only one, where human choice changes the outcome, and there are many. Because with human otherwise choice, compatibilism crumbles as a viable perspective of moral freedom because compatibilism does not permit any such state of affairs, whereas libertarian free will permits and even expects some events to be determined and some not to be determined. You may say you know compatibilists (Calvinists) who believe people have otherwise choice. While they may believe that (mix compatibilism and libertarianism), it is not what consistent Calvinism teaches, nor what is possible since compatibilism and libertarianism are mutually exclusive ideas. They simply do not understand compatibilism or consistent and developed Calvinism.

---

3. Good is used in the sense of civil good and not spiritual good (Rom 13:3).

7

Biblical Examples of God's Determinism and Man's Free Will

THIS TYPE OF PASSAGE is more common than we might think. We usually emphasize God's sovereignty in determining certain things, or we focus on a passage that clearly is about people making choices and the consequences of those. But many passages include both elements of determinism and libertarian free choice. I think that is probably true of everyday life as well. Consequently, some situations may include things determined and things that result from our choices. Passages with both determinism and libertarian freedom in the same event demonstrate how God not only created man with libertarian freedom but also how seamlessly determined actions and libertarian free choices relate to each other in God's plan.

The most dominant theme of Scripture is God. Second only to God is the plan of salvation. In salvation, we see the congruity of some things being determined with others that are not. For example, God chose to create the universe, to make man in his image, to permit man to sin, and, out of love, to provide salvation for all mankind. He determined what it would take to provide complete salvation and what it would take for man to be able to freely receive his salvation without being determined to do so. God determined he would do all the work of salvation and unconditionally provide it for all people. He further determined to condition the reception of salvation on grace-enabled faith. Even the grace to believe is unconditional, but believing is enabled by grace and required to receive salvation; the exercise of faith is man's part. Accordingly, the unconditional objective provision of salvation (Christ died for the sins of all, John 1:29) and the conditional subjective experience of salvation (Rom 10:9–10) seamlessly work together.

Genesis 1–2

We look at Genesis again, but this time our focus is on creation. The Bible begins with this profound statement. "In the beginning God created the heavens and the earth" (Gen 1:1). Out of nothing, God created all that was created. Human influence played no role in creation. We are created, which means we could not have created ourselves since we would need to exist before being created, which is an impossibility. God sovereignly chose out of his own prerogative to create. Man played no part in the initial creation, nor did he influence what would constitute creation.

God also determined man's role in creation, and this without any influence or merit of man. But God chose to give man a significant role in the operation of creation when he says mankind shall rule over the earth (Gen 1:26). Man did not play a part in influencing God's choice to create, what was created, or even his purpose for creating. Man did not even shape his role on the earth. The initial creation was a determined event.

But once man is placed in the garden of Eden, his libertarian freedom becomes evident. He is told that he can eat of every tree except one, and if he eats of that one, he will be punished by death (Gen 2:16–17). The warning clearly indicates a choice between eating and not eating. Notice, God solely determined the object and the choice that would demonstrate man's trust in God or himself. Man does not set or influence the criteria, but he clearly plays a decisive role in whether or not he would eat. Note again; man does not influence the consequence of eating. God sovereignly determined that eating would result in death; however, man was solely responsible for whether he would eat of the tree or not. Man did not have to eat, and he should not have eaten because to do so was to disobey the direct command of God.

God alone determined that none of his creation provided a suitable helper for Adam. He then chose to create a suitable helper without any influence or consultation from Adam regarding what the helper should look and be like (Gen 2:18, 20b–22). Adam played no part in the design of the helper. Amid God determining the need to create a special helper for Adam, he determined he would create the animal world and just what would constitute the animal world, and this without any consultation or influence from Adam (Gen 1:19–20a).

Once God sovereignly chose the composition of the animal kingdom, he sovereignly called Adam to name the various animals. This task appears to be Adam's first act in exercising his God-given ability to choose between options. Now I believe man being in God's image (Gen 1:26–27) is the first indicator of libertarian freedom along with God's commission for man and woman to "rule over" creation, which definitely involves making choices between options. But the first revealing act of libertarian freedom is in naming the animals. We read, "Out of the ground the Lord God formed every beast of the field and every bird of the sky, and brought them to the man to see what he would call them; and whatever the man called a living creature, that was its name" (Gen 2:19).

Notice the harmonious interplay between God determining what animals would exist and determining to bring the naming of the animals under the purview of Adam's rule. And that whatever Adam chose to name them, that is what they would be called. God delegated the task of animal naming to Adam, and Adam chose to accomplish that responsibility. It seems this, as well as cultivating the garden (Gen 2:15), is comprehended in the choice of God for humanity to "subdue" and "rule" (Gen 1:26–27).

Genesis makes it clear that man has free will to choose between accessible options, and God determines some things that are not influenced by man's choices, and both exist harmoniously throughout Scripture. As we shall see, this is what we often find in Scripture; that determinism and libertarian freedom exist in the same passage and even the same verse at times (Gen 2:19). Calvinists are often prone to see the entire passage in which something is determined as teaching that everything there is determined, which is consistent with Calvinism but not the Scripture.

God's creation leaves us with a great lesson. Some things are determined by God alone, and some things God decided to come about by the choices of man in which man could have chosen differently than he did. When Calvinists show you verses that clearly depict God determining things, do not be alarmed because we believe that and that he also determined some things to be the result of man using his libertarian free will. But Calvinists do not agree with this belief if they are consistent.

This same great truth undergirds the existence and nature of prayer, particularly conditionals. That is to say, God determined some things to be changeable through prayer. He decided what he would permit to be altered, and he determined they would be altered if we made our requests known to him in prayer. As a result, we must be faithful to make our requests known to him if we desire all that God has for us.

1 Chronicles 28

This passage provides a beautiful mixture of things affected by people's choices and things that are determined by God. David is talking about building the temple. Verse 8 says, "So now, in the sight of all Israel, the assembly of the Lord, and in the hearing of our God, observe and seek after all the commandments of the Lord your God so that you may possess the good land and bequeath it to your sons after you forever." The challenge is to observe and seek after all the commandments of the Lord, but the people have to make a deliberate choice to do that. The "so that" tells why they would want to choose to obey, which is to possess the land and pass it on to their sons. It is conditional. In other words, possessing the land is conditioned on their choice to observe all the Lord's commands.

It is evident that the consequence of not choosing to obey is they will not possess the land, and they will not be able to bequeath it to their sons. Consequently, the choice was clear. Choose to obey and get the land. Choose not to obey and do not get the land. If God predetermined their choice, hopefully, we can see and realize how nonsensical and meaningless all of this is. And if God had determined, in these passages and countless others, that the people could only choose to serve him or could only choose not to serve him, why give all these commands and warnings and promises? Why mislead people with conditional statements and commands when nothing is conditional or changeable? Not only would God be deluding us in life by giving us an undeniable sense that being human entails that we can make choices in which we could have chosen otherwise, but also it would mean that most of his holy word would be misleading since this type of scenario is ubiquitous in Scripture. This clarification reminds us that our view of man's moral freedom is really about our view of God, who created man.

Verse 9, "As for you, my son Solomon, know the God of your father, and serve Him with a whole heart and a willing mind; for the Lord searches all hearts, and understands every intent of the thoughts. If you seek Him, He will let you find Him; but if you forsake Him, He will reject you forever." Can you serve God without your whole heart? Yes. Not in a way that honors him because it is only outward serving. But even when we seek to serve him with our whole heart and a willing mind, that level of serving is most consistently revealed in our lives as we grow in Christ. We see this all the time, experientially speaking, whether in our own lives or others' lives. He says to serve with a willing mind, which includes being mentally aware and making a conscious and thoughtful choice. Sometimes we seek to serve God but lack a fully willing mind to serve him in whatever circumstance and way he desires. We have a willing mind to serve him where we are, but maybe not in, say, Africa. All of this is a matter of choice.

To serve him without reservation or with reservation is a choice we must make. The Lord searches and understands all of our hearts. God knows what we are thinking, what we are deliberating, and what we will freely choose. And he knows what we would have chosen had we chosen differently. He knows this for every single person on the planet. David tells Solomon not to just serve God in what can be seen by man because God looks beyond the actions into his heart, mind, and will.

It is a warning to all not to just go through the motions of Bible study, giving, worshiping, prayer, and devotionals because God is not looking at only the outward appearance. He is probing deeply inside of us and searching the very thoughts and intentions of our hearts (1 Sam 16:7). If we find ourselves going through the motions, we need to stop and confess it. We must bring our hearts and wills into line because God already knows they are not. God is not impressed with externals, just the heart and the will. He searches the intent of our thoughts. Recognizing we are not right with God and confessing it is a choice that is not determined. If it is determined, then the commands to confess our sins are nonsensical because the God who gave the command determined you to remain with unconfessed sin in your life.

Notice the "if" when David says, "If you seek Him, He will let you find Him; but if you forsake Him, He will reject you forever." These commands include clear choices made up of two conditionals that are laid before Solomon. Each conditional has equally clear consequences. That is to say, the nature of otherwise choice is that each option comes with its own set of consequences. If you seek him, Solomon (although you might not), you will find him. This is similar to verse 7, where God promised the continuance of Solomon's throne on the condition "if he resolutely performs My commandments and My ordinances." David makes a similar charge and challenge for all the people to seek God (v. 8), reminding them that the success of the Davidic dynasty now in the hands of Solomon depends on them all. Their faithfulness to God or lack thereof affects the future of the kingdom; this is clearly conditional.

Again, we see a passage in which some things are determined. They are not influenced by human involvement. Such as David not being able to build the temple, and God choosing Solomon to be the one because God did not want a warrior like David to build his temple despite David's desire and intention to be the one who built the temple (vv. 2–3). God chose David to be king and Judah to lead (v. 4), and out of David's many sons, God chose Solomon to be king (v. 5) and Solomon to build the temple (v. 6). Verse 10 coalesces the determined parts with the conditional saying, "Consider now, for the Lord has chosen you to build a house for the sanctuary; be courageous and act." There is the assurance in all of this that if Solomon seeks God, God will let him find him (v. 9) in tandem with a warning that if he does not, God will forsake him (v. 9).

The question is whether or not this passage's portrayal of multiple conditional statements is a series of real choices between accessible options or merely cryptic language to conceal God's determinism of every detail. Each reader must decide. The straightforward reading of the passage is that Solomon had to choose; each choice had a consequence, and he could have chosen either option. In the Bible, as in real life, if people are not choosing between accessible options, communication is unintelligible, and the life that we think we are living in which we make real choices and could have chosen differently is an illusion. If we are reading countless Scriptures throughout God's word and correctly concluding they are offering a choice when they are actually using language to conceal a determinative plan in which we all think we are reading and making actual choices, but we are not; that is cruel insanity created and perpetuated by God. But it is evident that Scripture's depiction of humanity having the ability and responsibility to choose what is right and reject what is wrong is what it appears to be. It is a choice between accessible options rather than a deceptive plan of God to make us think we can choose when we cannot because he determined *everything*. Calvinism's determinism distorts Scripture.

Verse 10, "Consider now, for the Lord has chosen you to build a house for the sanctuary; be courageous and act." This sentence beautifully coalesces the passage's determined components and those allowing the free will of man. God chose Solomon over David or any of David's other offspring to build the temple. There is no human involvement in this decision. But, the part that involves human choice is for the temple to be built by Solomon;

he must "be courageous and act." God knows what Solomon will do. Therefore, he is not surprised by Solomon's actions. Neither is his knowledge of Solomon's actions causal. That is clear from all of the conditionals in this passage, including the charge to "be courageous and act," which is only meaningful if contrasted with the idea that if you do not courageously act, you will not build the temple or continue to reign (v. 7).

Matthew 1:19–20

This passage contains aspects that are unaffected by human choice. At the same time, it includes components that are only certain because they involve humans' choices that make a real difference. This passage is about the birth of Christ. It tells us the Messiah would enter into this world at a specific time and in a particular way determined by God apart from human influence. However, the actual birth did involve some choices by the individuals involved. Matt 1:19–20 says that Joseph "planned to send her away. . . . But when he had considered this, behold, an angel of the Lord appeared to him in a dream, saying, 'Joseph, son of David, do not be afraid to take Mary as your wife; for the Child who has been conceived in her is of the Holy Spirit.'" The words "planned" and "considered" indicate a deliberative choice. Planned means "to think, with the purpose of planning or deciding on a course of action—to purpose, to plan, to intend."[1] And the word considered (v. 20) means "to process information by giving consideration to various aspects—to think about, to consider."[2] The idea of choice and consequence permeates the pages of Scripture. Everything being predetermined does not work in the passages we have looked at and countless other passages. These few are illustrative but not in any way exhaustive. For God to predetermine people to sin and rebel, and then judge them for doing what he unalterably designed them to do, if not so eternally serious, would be cartoonish if true. In contrast, it is quite easy to understand if he gives man the freedom and ability to choose between right and wrong. And if people choose to obey, they are blessed, and if they choose to disobey, they are punished. Like the passages in which God repeatedly taught people to choose righteousness, we find Jesus taught people and the disciples to choose righteousness repetitively. He teaches us that way because he does not want us to fall under his judgment. As stated earlier, man after the fall

1. Louw and Nida, *Greek-English Lexicon*, 356.
2. Louw and Nida, *Greek-English Lexicon*, 348–49.

does not initiate a relationship with God; God does by his redemption plan in which he grace-enables fallen man and woman to be able to respond to him.

The examples we have seen demonstrate that man had a choice to follow or not follow God before sin entered the world because of God's creative grace. Following the fall, man has a choice to follow or not follow God because of redemptive grace. God is always calling people to choose to follow and serve him. Prayer is significantly related to God's call and enablement of man to choose. The choice to follow Christ is not singular. It begins with choosing to believe the gospel and is followed by choosing countless times to learn and obey his commands (Matt 28:18–20). The choice to believe in salvation and follow him daily is considerably dependent on man praying to God and God answering man's prayer.

8

Biblical Examples of People Choosing to Follow Christ before and after Salvation

As WE HAVE SEEN, we find people in Scripture making choices between accessible options before and after the fall regarding serving God or not serving God. We find events that are undeniably determined by God so that human involvement did not nor cannot affect them. We also have seen events in which there was a mixture of God determining certain aspects apart from human involvement in the same context as events that resulted from libertarian free choice. I trust you are beginning to see how choosing to pray or not pray and God's conditioning some outcomes on whether we pray or not is consistent with the way God designed man and woman and his interactions with them throughout the Scripture. This next set of passages is about New Testament gospel encounters and the Christian life that follows. The most important choice and prayer anyone ever makes is about trusting Christ as Savior. A study of prayer would be incomplete without considering the choices, requests, and prayers of the lost in salvation.

Mark 10:17–23

Mark records an incident between Jesus and the rich young ruler. Mark tells us, "As He was setting out on a journey, a man ran up to Him and knelt before Him, and asked Him, 'Good Teacher, what shall I do to inherit eternal life?'" (Mark 10:17). This question was also asked by the Philippian at the ruler's heart and gave him three commands—sell your po[...] give to the poor, and come and follow me. Jesus knew his heart [...] genuinely in love with God to be saved, and he had to be willing to do what Christ said for him to do. It is not that everyone must precisely do the first two of these commandments to be saved, but the essence of them must be present, which means to make Jesus first in our life. For someone else, it may be summarized by walking away from self-reliance of another sort. Whatever making Christ first in a person's life entails is what he must do. For me personally, I believed in God, but I had money first, family second, and God third. My salvation came with the realization that God must be first. In each case, it means to follow Christ and die to our own plans, governance, values, aspirations, and abilities. It is the call to take up our cross (Matt 16:24).

"But at these words he was saddened, and he went away grieving, for he was one who owned much property" (Mark 10:22). Notice the encounter, deliberation, choice, and emotions. The choice was to sell what he had and be devoted to Christ or keep all his wealth and continue to be religious. It was a call to follow Christ and be saved or continue to live for himself and be lost; he chose the latter. But everything indicates he heard and understood the commands, deliberated about the cost of following Christ, and he made a choice, which was not an easy one because knowing he had chosen to walk away from Christ left him sad. The word "sad" means "to be sad as the result of what has happened or what one has done—to be sad, to be distressed . . . greatly distressed."[1] His sadness was due to his choice in light of what he could have chosen. Not every choice is easy because not every choice is between only good results and bad results. Walking off from much is usually more difficult than walking off from little. Everything in the passage indicates a real choice was made between these two accessible options, and whatever he did choose, he could have chosen differently.

If a person believes in Calvinism's compatible determinism, on the one hand, you have the problem of Jesus salvifically loving the non-elect ruler and giving him commands that would lead to salvation. On the other hand, Jesus is the author of the plan that would not allow the ruler to experience what Christ was offering. There are two reasons why this is the case. One, because with compatible moral freedom, the ruler could only choose to do what he did. It is impossible, given the same past, that he could have chosen differently even though Jesus' words indicate that he could and should. Two, because the ruler walked away, we know he is one of the non-elect. To believe that Jesus would present salvation as attainable when he designed it so that the ruler *could not* choose to inherit eternal life is a ghastly suggestion emanating from beyond the text.

Some determinists seek to lessen Jesus' disingenuousness by saying, as a human, Jesus didn't know who were the elect. Therefore, Jesus presented what Calvinists call a good faith offer. But the good faith offer will not save Jesus from duplicity or deception if determinism is true because Jesus said he only did the will of the Father and spoke the words of the Father. "So Jesus said, 'When you lift up the Son of Man, then you will know that I am He, and I do nothing on My own initiative, but I speak these things as the Father taught Me'" (John 8:28; see also John 4:38; 5:19; 6:38; 12:49). The Father does know the salvation plan. If the unconditionally elect and the reprobates (those that God was pleased to damn without an opportunity for redemption) are determined, then you have the Father leading Jesus to speak things that cannot possibly happen, yet appearing that they could. Consistent Calvinism leads to a horrendous depiction of the Father and Son.

The passage seems to make it objectively clear why he did not come. It was because he had so much wealth, "he was one who owned much property" (v. 22, also 23, 25). Christ offered him "treasure in heaven" (v. 21), which would require faith and giving up his wealth in this life. He wanted

---

1. Louw and Nida, *Greek-English Lexicon*, 317.

to be a child of God on his terms. Not all people are called to give up all their wealth, but that does not mean we can come halfheartedly. In John's gospel, many were believing in and following Jesus, but Jesus did not commit himself to them because he knew they lacked true faith (John 2:23–24). When the miracles were interrupted by Jesus talking about his death, many of his disciples left him (John 6:66). As with Adam and Eve, the Israelites, Solomon, and this rich young ruler, God is looking for one thing; that we seek him with our whole heart and make him first in our lives. There is no sense in which this passage suggests the young ruler did not come because he was not one of the elect. Instead, it was because he chose his wealth over the wealth of heaven, which by every contextual indication, he could have chosen.

To further confuse the issue, the determinist might say he agrees that the young man turned away because he chose his wealth over the treasure of Christ and what he offered. He will say the young man rejected the call of Christ to follow him because of his wealth, but what that actually means is that his riches were a secondary cause of his rejection. What the Calvinist does not tell you is that according to compatibilism and unconditional election, the truth is the man would not believe because he *could* not believe: he was not one of God's elect. This belief includes the truth of compatibilism that while he freely chose to reject the offer of Christ, he could not have chosen differently than he did, given the same past. The nature of compatibilism and unconditional election is that God is the ultimate cause of the man's disbelief, and, according to compatibilism, the young man was the proximate cause of disbelief (the closest cause to the event). God is the ultimate reason he did not get saved because if this man were one of the elect, he would have.

Therefore, that he chose his wealth over the wealth of Christ is only trivially true. In other words, yes, according to Calvinism, he did choose his wealth over Christ's wealth. But the reason he did so was not that he chose between accessible options, but because of compatibilism, he could not have chosen otherwise, and God did not choose him for salvation. Accordingly, our clarifying question for the determinist would be, do you believe that specific man, in the moral moment of decision, could have chosen to follow Jesus or chosen not to follow, and whatever he did choose, he could have chosen differently? His answer will be no if he understands compatibilism and speaks consistently with Calvinism's determinism.

The Bible often states the cause for faith or lack of faith, for choosing righteousness or choosing sin, for believing in Christ or choosing not to believe in Christ, as it does in this passage. If he did not believe because of his compatible moral freedom and, therefore, could not believe or he was not elect, the Bible is capable of saying that, but it did not. We should trust the Bible and not read our system into the otherwise clear teaching of Scripture.[2]

I want to quote a compatibilist, a Calvinist, a wonderful man of God, and founder of Dallas Theological Seminary, Lewis Sperry Chafer. This quote is an example of how difficult determinism is to detect in much of Calvinists' writings.

Chafer writes, "Transforming things mighty indeed are wrought by prayer. But only such things as comport with the will and the purpose of God. Why then should prayer be offered? Only because of the fact that the divine purpose, which the answer to prayer represents, includes the prayer feature. It is as much decreed that it shall be done in answer to prayer as it is decreed that it shall be done at all."[3] At first glance, you say prayer does mighty things; praise God! Once you look at the language he uses and understand he is speaking from a determinist perspective, you realize the word "decreed" means it is the way it is, and it could not have been any different. It is virtually the same as determined. The answer to the prayer could not have been different; the work of God could not have been different. The person who prayed it could not have prayed differently, and the person who didn't pray it could not have chosen to pray.

As a consistent Calvinist (although he speaks inconsistently at times), Chafer would have to believe everything is micro-determined. And since everything is determined, he seeks to answer the question that naturally arises. Why pray? What is his answer? It is we only pray because prayer is a *feature* of God's determined plan. It doesn't change anything one way or the other. It is simply a feature of the plan. The prayer, the person praying,

---

2. Another way to express this is as follows. The passage makes it appear that his unwillingness to walk away from his wealth was the paramount and only true reason he walked away, whereas if determinism and unconditional election are true, the paramount reason he walked away is because God determined him to be one of the non-elect, a reprobate; therefore, he walked away because he was predetermined to do so. Hence, his wealth is a trivial matter in his decision to reject salvation. Trivial in the sense that he could not have chosen to walk away from his wealth because he was determined to walk away from Christ.

3. Chafer, *Systematic Theology*, 1:256.

and the words of the prayer are all determined as is the person who does not pray. The decreed will of God is that he determined A to happen and just as determinatively decreed someone to pray for A to happen. But A does not happen because someone prayed who could have prayed for A or B to happen. Nor does it mean the person could not have prayed for A, and A would not have happened. In Calvinism, the person was decreed to pray at that time, saying precisely what he said because that is what God determined to happen.

But as we read Scripture, it does appear that some situations are determined, even as it equally appears that some events are affected by human choice and prayer and are, therefore, not determined. These events or outcomes are the results of libertarian free choice; as a result, they are contingencies, indefinite events, because their coming into existence is contingent on the person with libertarian free will choosing to so act. Accordingly, as we have seen, we find many conditional statements and commands in Scripture.

What should we do about things that are undetermined or incidents about which we are unsure whether they are determined or undetermined? We should pray! It seems safe to assume that in areas beyond where Scripture speaks specifically, there are many events God has determined to happen in a precise way, time, and for a precise purpose. It also seems equally safe to assume he has made many conditionals as he did in Scripture.

In other words, they will come about one way if we do not ask or pray and another if we do. How they turn out is contingent on what we do. Although it may be possible to deduce some things that exist beyond Scripture that are determined, it is probably best to pray since we cannot know for sure. Because they may be conditionals, and as with the conditionals in Scripture, God has designed them to be affected by human involvement of exercising choice, one of which is to pray.

Mark 6:1–6

Christ performing miracles gives us another glimpse into the area of choice and determinism. Mark says,

> Jesus went out from there and came into His hometown; and His disciples followed Him. When the Sabbath came, He began to teach in the synagogue; and the many listeners were astonished, saying, "Where did this man get these things, and what is this

wisdom given to Him, and such miracles as these performed by His hands? Is not this the carpenter, the son of Mary, and brother of James and Joses and Judas and Simon? Are not His sisters here with us?" And they took offense at Him. Jesus said to them, "A prophet is not without honor except in his hometown and among his own relatives and in his own household." And He could do no miracle there except that He laid His hands on a few sick people and healed them. And He wondered at their unbelief. And He was going around the villages teaching. (Mark 6:1–6)

Jesus had been performing many miracles, but when he arrives at his own hometown, Mark said, "He could do no miracle there," except heal a few sick people. This statement raises the question. As deity, did he not have the power to do miracles? Yes, he did. Did he lose it for a moment? No, he did not. Then why could he not do more miracles there? It is very clearly stated that it is because of their unbelief. Matthew says, "And He did not do many miracles there because of their unbelief" (Matt 13:58). We often see this type of conditional in passages that speak about salvation, serving God, and prayer. Jesus did miracles that were proportional to and conditioned on their faith. Jesus had not lost the power to do miracles, but in God's plan, there were times when it mattered what the people among whom he was working believed. Accordingly, as a servant to the will of the Father, Jesus could only perform miracles proportionate to the faith of the people.

James A. Brooks says, "God and his Son could do anything, but they have chosen to limit themselves in accordance to human response."[4] John D. Grassmick comments, "There was no limitation on His power, but His purpose was to perform miracles in the presence of faith. Only a few here had faith to come to Him for healing."[5] As a result, the number and kind of miracles and healings were conditional. God designed Christ's working of miracles, at least some of the time, to be contingent on the level of faith of the people.

In Nazareth, he did little because of their little faith, and Jesus *wondered* at their unbelief. Jesus was here to do the will of the Father, and as salvation is by faith, at times, God restricted Christ's miracle-working ministry to reflect the level of faith that was present. Jesus was doing the will and work of the Father. Jesus said, "Truly, truly, I say to you, the Son can do nothing of Himself, unless it is something He sees the Father doing; for

4. Brooks, *Mark*, 100.
5. Grassmick, "Mark," 127.

whatever the Father does, these things the Son also does in like manner" (John 5:19).

If Jesus did only the work of the Father and only spoke the words of the Father (John 3:34; 8:28; 12:50), why would he "wonder at their unbelief" if God predetermined everyone who would believe? If they could have only little belief or massive unbelief because the Father determined that, then why would Christ be astonished at the level of their disbelief? A Calvinist might say, in Christ's humanity, he did not know all things, and so as a human, when he experienced their determined lack of faith, it astonished him. I would say it seems more likely that he was negatively astonished because, as the redeemer, he knew they had enough evidence and the ability to understand who he was and believe, but they chose not to believe. Christ's response to the people was conditioned on their faith, or lack thereof, just like salvation.

John 12:35–36

This passage says, "So Jesus said to them, 'For a little while longer the Light is among you. Walk while you have the Light, so that darkness will not overtake you; he who walks in the darkness does not know where he goes. While you have the Light, believe in the Light, so that you may become sons of Light.' These things Jesus spoke, and He went away and hid Himself from them" (John 12:35–36).

We see six things in this encounter with the gospel. First, note the presence of the light, which is the only time someone can believe unto salvation. Second, observe that the presence of the light is not enough to result in salvation. It is necessary for salvation but not sufficient. Third, they have to obey the commands to "walk" and "believe" while they have the light. Fourth, notice the urgency. They have to believe while they have the light, which they only have for a little while. Fifth, witness the power of the light. The power of the light of Christ, the gospel, can penetrate the darkness cast by sin, evil, and Satan's blinders.

A person can come out of the darkness of sin, but only when the light is there because man is no match for the power of sin and Satan. Sixth, we see the reason for the gospel. If they walk and believe while they have the light, they are promised that the darkness will not overtake them. Jesus says, "So that you may become sons of light." They can become Christians and never be enslaved by sin and darkness again. Christ does all the work so man can believe and be in a relationship with him, just as he did all the work in the first creation. While they are in the darkness of sin, they are to receive the light that is given, or the darkness will overcome them again. The darkness is held in abeyance while the light of the gospel is present. If they do not receive the light of the gospel, when the light is withdrawn, they are overtaken by darkness again.

Thus, Christ has done all the work of the gospel, even grace enabling people by the power of the gospel light to have an opportunity to become Christians so that the darkness they have been temporarily delivered from will not again overtake them. But, they must choose to believe. Exercising faith is God's designed condition to receive salvation (John 3:18; Rom 4:2–5).

Colossians 3:10–16

This passage is about our Christian walk. It highlights how our choices affect our Christian walk. Paul says, "Let the peace of Christ rule in your hearts, to which indeed you were called in one body; and be thankful" (Col 3:15). They had been reconciled with God in salvation (Rom 5:10), and, as a result, they are no longer enemies with God but his children (Eph 5:1). Even though they are born again, true believers who follow Christ, they are commanded to "let the peace of Christ rule in your hearts." Rule is a command in the original and means to let preside or arbitrate. More specifically, the Holy Spirit says you are commanded to let the peace of Christ preside in your heart and life. Added to that, because Christ has called them into one body, they are commanded to be thankful. That can be translated to show themselves thankful or become thankful. In both instances, there is a command to be obeyed and a choice of whether to obey or not.

There are three reasons why we know this is not something that is determined. One, it is a command. The very nature of a command is that a person must choose whether to obey or not, as we saw in the first command with Adam and Eve. Two, it is meaningless to command people to act like they are already inviolably determined to act or not to act.[6] We know by observation and testimonies that not all Christians walk in the peace of Christ. Quite unfortunately, I dare say, if we did not know that about others, we know it about ourselves. Three, we have every reason to recognize

---

6. See Appendix 1 for my response to Calvinism's contention that it is logical to command someone to do what they cannot do.

a causal relationship between our desire and our choice to so walk or not walk, lest all relational actions are a big delusion orchestrated by God. It is a choice, just like the choice to be saved. The Christian life is all about choices, and every choice has consequences.

It is important to remember that the unflinching micro-determinism of compatibilism does not become less deterministic once a person is saved. It is the same. According to compatibilism, if a person is walking in the peace of Christ, it is because God determined him to do so, and he cannot choose otherwise. Conversely, if he is not walking in the peace of God, it is because God determined that he did not do so, and he cannot choose otherwise. That is the nature of compatibilism, which makes nonsense of all the commands for discipleship, spiritual growth, faithfulness, serving, and every other area.[7] The provision is there, but it is not forced on the believer. It is available to those who choose to obey the command. For those who do not, there is anxiety. We have the peace of salvation through grace-enabled faith, and now that same grace grants us the opportunity to walk in peace or not to walk in peace.

1 Thessalonians 5:13

This passage provides another straightforward example of libertarian freedom. "But we request of you, brethren, that you appreciate those who diligently labor among you, and have charge over you in the Lord and give you instruction, and that you esteem them very highly in love because of their work. Live in peace with one another" (1 Thess 5:12–13). Paul asks the Thessalonians to appreciate and esteem those who labor among them, lead them, and give them instruction. If this is an outcome that is determined, it seems rather pointless and misleading to request they do this. I dare say, no one could glean determinism from the verses themselves; if it is here, it is artificially superimposed. I believe anyone reading the passage would normally understand it to say that Paul requested something of them and hoped and believed they would so choose, but they surely did not have to choose according to Paul's request.

The phrase *live in peace with one another* is a plural command. Accordingly, the command is given to all who are in the church at Thessalonica.

---

7. To better understand why the Calvinists' claim that humans have compatible freedom at certain times and libertarian freedom at others is flawed and impossible, see *Does God Love All or Some?*, chapter 6, under "Total Depravity."

The very nature of a command is that one should do it, is obligated to do it, but may choose to disobey, precisely what we see throughout Scripture and everyday life. What then is the point of God giving commands to people he has predetermined not to be able to obey? He does not need more evidence that we are all sinners and deserve hell. He does not need to make sure some do not obey, and therefore he guarantees it by determining it because the truth is that libertarian free will can assure us that there will be sufficient numbers of people who do not obey. I hope you can see that the brush of determinism paints a warped portrait of God.

Just a normal reading of the passage clearly sets forth a choice. While they can choose not to dwell in peace, they can and should choose to obey the command and walk in peace. That God commands them to do what brings him glory and blesses them is true to the biblical portrait of God, who is holy love and loving righteousness. However, if determinism is true, you have God Almighty, who says he loves the ones he commands to do what he has predetermined they can never do as much as he loves the ones he determined to obey his every command. Repeatedly, we are led to understand the two perspectives regarding the nature of man's moral freedom are never ultimately about our view of man but always reflective of our view of who God is and what we believe about God.

9

Biblical Examples of God Rewarding and Judging People's Choices

Matthew 19:27–30

GOD REWARDS SACRIFICIAL CHOICES. Throughout the Scriptures, God gives man a choice between various options with concomitant consequences corresponding to the choice made. Here is an example involving Simon Peter.

> Then Peter said to Him, "Behold, we have left everything and followed You; what then will there be for us?" And Jesus said to them, "Truly I say to you, that you who have followed Me, in the regeneration when the Son of Man will sit on His glorious throne, you also shall sit upon twelve thrones, judging the twelve tribes of Israel. And everyone who has left houses or brothers or sisters or father or mother or children or farms for My name's sake, will receive many times as much, and will inherit eternal life. But many who are first will be last; and the last, first." (Matt 19:27–30)

The context of this encounter follows immediately after Jesus' encounter with the rich young ruler in which the ruler chose not to walk away from everything he had to follow Jesus (Matt 19:21–22). Now Peter is wondering about the disciples who did walk off from everything to follow Christ (Matt 4:18–22; 9:9). This question is not just for the apostles. As followers of Christ, I assume we all have asked this type of question. If you sacrifice things in this world and walk the path of faith and insecurity (humanly speaking), this question comes up. At least it has for me.

Peter questioned if the rich young ruler would not leave his wealth and security to follow you, and we have, what will be the difference for us? Recognizing the contextual contrast of the rich young ruler's decision and the apostle's decision highlights the conditional nature of the passage, the choice to follow Christ or not, and the consequences of that choice. The rich young ruler chose to walk away, and by so doing, he kept his earthly wealth but lost eternal life and treasures in heaven. Whereas the apostles chose to walk away from their earthly wealth, and Jesus promises what they will receive because of that decision.

It is all about choice. Jesus promises the apostles that in the regeneration, which is the rebirth of everything at his second coming and ultimately the new heaven and earth (Matt 19:28–30; Acts 3:21), they will sit on thrones, judging the twelve tribes of Israel. That is a specific promise for answering the call of Christ to follow him in salvation as an apostle. That particular reward is limited to them. But Christ expands the promise to bless all who choose to become his followers when he says, "And everyone who has left houses or brothers or sisters or father or mother or children or farms for My name's sake, will receive many times as much, and will inherit eternal life" (Matt 19:29). Some of the rewards may be experienced in this life as well (Mark 10:30).

It is a choice of faith to trust Christ for salvation. This choice is multiplied many times when he asks us as we follow him to leave the securities of this life to go where he is leading. We may lose everything, and we may even lose it several times. We follow because he is worthy of being followed and because he promises to take care of us. But notice he goes beyond necessary provision. He promises we receive eternal life and many times more than we ever sacrificed in following him. But, to receive the rewards, we must choose to trust him because we may lose much before the promise is fulfilled. The phrase "many who are first will be last; and the last, first" seems to be related to the equality of salvation as seen in the following parable. While there are rewards for faithful service promised in Scripture, there is an equality of salvation. The apostles received the same eternal life as the thief on the cross.

Matthew 21:33–46

God judges selfish choices as well. The parable of the landowner in Matt 21:33–46 is an example of this truth. The landowner planted a vineyard and then rented it out. He sent his slave to collect the rent, and renters killed the slave. He sent another slave, and they killed him too. Finally, the landowner said he will send his son and thinks surely, they will respect and pay him. Jesus makes very clear at the end of this parable that he is referring to the Pharisees. God gave the leaders of Israel the land, God sent his prophets, and the leaders killed them. He then sent more prophets, and the leaders killed them.

Regarding the son, it says,

> But afterward he sent his son to them, saying, "They will respect my son." But when the vine-growers saw the son, they said among themselves, "This is the heir; come, let us kill him and seize his inheritance." They took him, and threw him out of the vineyard and killed him. Therefore when the owner of the vineyard comes, what will he do to those vine-growers? They said to Him, "He will bring those wretches to a wretched end, and will rent out the vineyard to other vine-growers who will pay him the proceeds at the proper seasons." Jesus said to them, "Did you never read in the Scriptures, 'The stone which the builders rejected, This became the chief corner stone; This came about from the Lord, And it is marvelous in our eyes?' Therefore I say to you, the kingdom of God will be taken away from you and given to a people, producing the fruit of it. And he who falls on this stone will be broken to pieces; but on whomever it falls, it will scatter him like dust." When the chief priests and the Pharisees heard His parables, they understood that He was speaking about them. (Matt 21:37–45)

This passage not only demonstrates a conditional, something that could have been different had the renters chosen differently, but it allows us a glimpse into the deliberative process of the renters. Notice the choice and the deliberation among various people. The vine-growers deliberated together to plan what, how, and whom of the vine-growers would join in on the plan (vv. 35–36). Then, with the plan in place, when the landowner sent his son, they talked and agreed, as a group, to "seize his inheritance" (Matt 21:38). Their ultimate goal to seize the land is now evident.

Several choices were made before the final choice to kill the son, and the deliberative process is evident. This process is precisely what one would expect from a libertarian free will encounter, including choices, deliberation, and consequences.[1] It does not reflect compatible moral freedom in

1. Compatibilism permits experiential (subjective) deliberation but not objective. That is to say, if compatibilism is true, one can have the experience he is choosing

which they could not have chosen differently. Actually, the landowner expected them to act differently, particularly regarding his son (v. 37). From a compatible perspective, everything was determined; they were determined by God to steal and kill, and the landowner was determined to trust them and think they would respect his son. But the truth is that this passage does not even hint at determinism, which actually turns a tragic situation in which God severely judges people for doing evil into a cosmic puppet show. This passage speaks of a choice and a consequential judgment. The choice is always connected to the consequence, whether the consequence is reward or judgment. And we all understand it that way.

It concludes with this, "When the chief priests and the Pharisees heard His parables, they understood that He was speaking about them. When they sought to seize Him, they feared the people, because they considered Him to be a prophet" (Matt 21:45–46).

---

between options and could choose differently than he chooses, but it is not objective deliberation because he cannot actually choose differently. Libertarian freedom includes an objective deliberative process.

10

Biblical Examples of Our Choice in Prayer

STARTING WITH THIS CHAPTER, we will look at verses that specifically deal with prayer. I want to focus on conditional prayers and what it means to pray conditional prayers, and what it means if we do not pray them. In the context of prayer, the outcome of conditional prayers is dependent on asking God in prayer. Resultantly, if we pray, the outcome will probably be different than if we do not pray. Scripture emphasizes praying, and conditional prayers are vital to experiencing daily fellowship and an intimate walk with God. As I pray you will see, there does not seem to be a limit to the number of conditionals we might experience in a day, which means that we should be praying for all things all the time, or else we will miss much of what God desires to do in and through us.

John 14:13–14

As Jesus was nearing the end of his earthly ministry, *The Bible Knowledge Commentary* sums up the context and mood, saying, "The disciples were completely bewildered and discouraged. Jesus had said He was going away (7:34; 8:21; 12:8, 35; 13:33), that He would die (12:32–33), that one of the Twelve was a traitor (13:21), that Peter would disown Him three times (13:38), that Satan was at work against all of them (Luke 22:31–32), and that all the disciples would fall away (Matt. 26:31). The cumulative weight of these revelations must have greatly depressed them."[1] In that context,

1. Blum, "John," 322.

Jesus begins to set forth guidance and encouragement regarding what they had heard and experienced in light of the fact that they would no longer have Christ physically with them. Jesus told the disciples, who were greatly grieved about his departure (John 16:20–22), "Whatever you ask in My name, that will I do, so that the Father may be glorified in the Son. If you ask Me anything in My name, I will do it" (John 14:13–14). This promise does not seem to be restricted to just the twelve. Just before these words, he says, "Truly, truly, I say to you, he who believes in Me, the works that I do, he will do also; and greater works than these he will do; because I go to the Father" (John 14:12). The "he who believes in Me" expands the audience beyond the twelve. To do greater works is a promise for all who believe and serve Christ, which necessitates the opportunity for all to pray and experience answered prayer.

Christ further shows that he is speaking about more than what the Father and he will do for the twelve when he says, "I will ask the Father, and He will give you another Helper, that He may be with you forever" (John 14:16). He did not limit giving the Holy Spirit to the apostles but to all believers (Acts 2:38; Rom 5:5; 1 Cor 6:19). Additionally, the pronoun "you" is plural (John 14:12–15), which signifies he is at least speaking to the disciples, but can include others as well. Christ says, "If you love me, you will keep my commandments" (John 14:15), and that is true of all who claim to know Christ, not just the apostles. If it were not for these verses, there might be merit in concluding this promise is only for the apostles, but they make it clear this is for all who follow Christ. And so, we should be making our requests known to the Father through prayer in Jesus' name so that he can be glorified.

Our prayers and the answers provided by Christ are to glorify the Father, which is consistent with all Scripture that everything is to glorify God (Matt 5:16; Rom 15:6; 1 Cor. 6:20; 10:31). We glorify God when we make our requests known, asking God for what is on our hearts. This being true, if we do not bring our needs, desires, wants, and all things we think we need to faithfully serve God, as well as what we think he may want to do in our lives, he cannot be fully glorified in the sense that he will not answer what we do not ask. Our ultimate purpose in all things is to glorify God. If we do not pray and make our requests known, the Father is not glorified because we are not following his instructions to pray and ask. He cannot be glorified through answered prayer if we do not pray and make our requests known.

A word about followers of Christ doing "greater works" (v. 12) than Christ is in order. That is best understood to mean greater quantitatively, not qualitatively. Gerald Borchert notes, "It should be noted at the outset, however, that 'greater' can hardly here mean that believers will do more dramatic works than the raising of Lazarus (11:43–44), the changing of water to wine (2:7–11), the walking on the Sea of Galilee (6:19), the multiplying of loaves and fish (6:9–14), or any of the other amazing acts of Jesus."[2] There is nothing any of us can do collectively that is greater than Christ because he is the one who took away the sin of the world (John 1:29) and is the Savior of the world (Acts 4:42).

What Christ began in advancing the kingdom, he will now do through his people, and much of that is dependent on prayer. While the normal way of praying is to the Father through Jesus' name (vv. 13, 14; 16:23), we can also pray to Jesus (v. 14). Obviously, whatever and anything are not absolute. This is irrefutable since we know he is not going to grant a request for sin or things that would ultimately thwart his salvation plan. That does not mean the words are not exceedingly inclusive. As we seek to follow Christ's word, life, example, and the Holy Spirit's leading into the precise subjective path he has for us as individuals, the things we will need to pray for are innumerable. Add to that the things God may bring into our lives to enhance our experiential trust and relationship with him. When you think of all the things God might do in and through us, and all that is needed on our journey to be faithful, the list of things to pray about is gargantuan. Additionally, while God may provide minimally at times for greater spiritual purposes of which we are unaware, he is not a minimalist by nature.

Now note the sentence structure is very down-to-earth. It is conditional. The promises are "that I will do" and "I will do it," but there is a condition to be met. The promises only apply "if we ask." If we do not ask, we may safely assume there are untold numbers of things God wants to do in and through us that we will never experience. It is like the verse, "If you love Me, you will keep My commandments" (John 14:15). The condition to meet is to love Christ (if you love me), and the test of our love is measured by our desire to keep his commandments.

Verse 15 is a parallel statement to the guidelines for prayer in verse 14. "If you love me" and "if you ask me anything in my name." If someone really loves Christ, his heart will be to keep Christ's commandments. And if someone asks in Christ's name, consistent with who Christ is, the promise

2. Borchert, *John 12–21*, 115.

is that Christ will do it. Thus, if we ask, he will do it, and if we love him, we will do it. Another way to see this is, if we do not ask, he will not give, and if we do not love him, we do not obey. Loving Christ includes obeying Scripture to confess our sins (1 John 1:9), similarly praying according to God's will includes making our requests known.

Christ makes it unmistakably understandable. If we do not ask, Christ will not do what he would do if we ask. I think we can know this by a simple consideration. If he will do it even if we do not ask, what is the point of asking? If the condition doesn't make a difference in the outcome, then don't worry about it. An unconditional condition is meaningless.

Additionally, if everything is determined, it is what it is, and everything is exactly as God determined it to be. But if it is genuinely conditional, as it seems to be, then if you do not ask, Christ does not do it. If you do not love him, you will not keep his commandments. But if you do ask, he will do it; the promise is automatic when the condition is met.

After considering these verses for a few years, now, when I see something or have a thought about something, I seek to remember to ask. Sometimes I may have an explicit Scripture regarding the prayer request, while at other times, I do not, but I do have a biblical principle to guide me. Often, I am not sure whether what I am praying about that is not an explicit conditional in Scripture is still included as a conditional in the commands to pray about "everything." It could be something God has determined to be. But I pray because I would rather ask and get turned down than not ask and miss something God has for me. If our hearts are to do the will of God, both objectively (Scripture) and subjectively (what he wants to do in us and through us personally), then I believe we should err on the side of asking rather than not asking. I say this in the context of always seeking to know Christ and his word better.

As with all prayer, my secure resting place is found in my deepest desire, "Your will be done." As he said, we ask, and we can only do so according to our understanding at that particular moment in our spiritual growth. But we are safe from missing God's best when we say and mean, "Your will be done." This request practically means, Lord, I have asked as you said; I have done so to the best of my understanding, but please know I trust you more than me. I want your will if it is what I have prayed, and even if it is the direct opposite. I want you to override my request and do what would be your perfect will for that brings you glory and is, in the end, best for me. I trust you!

It is essential to understanding prayer and living in God's will that we must ask in prayer for all things. We cannot just think that praying "Your will be done" covers everything, for how could it since Scripture explicitly commands that we ask in prayer so he can answer through Jesus and be glorified? To say it another way, praying "Your will be done" is not a short-cut for making all our requests known through prayer. To use it as such is to not pray in the will of God because we are bypassing his express will to make our requests known to him. It is not our pass to not ask, seek, knock, and believe; rather, it is our rest and security (Matt 7:7; Mark 11:24; Phil 4:6).

John 16:23–24

This is similar to the previous verses. Here Jesus said, "In that day you will not question Me about anything. Truly, truly, I say to you, if you ask the Father for anything in My name, He will give it to you. Until now you have asked for nothing in My name; ask and you will receive, so that your joy may be made full" (John 16:23–24). Jesus is talking about the future when he will no longer be with them physically. While he was with them physically, they would most frequently pose their questions to him (Matt 13:10; 14:13; Acts 1:6). He is preparing them to make their requests known to the Father. In order to follow Christ, serve God, and live a faithful life after Jesus' death, burial, resurrection, and ascension, they would need to go to the Father for their requests.

Up to this point, they had not asked anything in Jesus' name, but when Jesus is no longer physically with them, they would. This passage teaches Christians to pray in the name of Jesus. Although the loss of Jesus' presence would foster confusion and sadness, they are to be encouraged because that will turn to joy as they begin to relate to the Father through Jesus in this new way. The Father will meet their needs in ways that will bring great joy to their lives, regardless of the circumstances.

When we combine the previous prayer and this one, two purposes emerge. First, Christ will answer prayers "so that the Father may be glorified in the Son" (John 14:13). Second, he will answer prayers "so that your joy may be made full" (John 16:24). Christ wants the disciples to ask so he can answer their prayers so that the Father can continue to be glorified through him, and the disciples can continue to serve him in joy even though he will be physically absent. For the moment, they were deeply grieved, but prayer would be a significant way for Jesus to bring joy into their hearts. By application, the same is true of us as well. Note that asking in prayer for things so that we may walk in true joy is not in conflict with God being glorified.

Consider the original creation and the environment in which God placed Adam and Eve. It went far beyond their basic needs. God created a beautiful environment and structured fulfilling tasks to increase their pleasure in the garden. He removed man's loneliness (Gen 2:18) and said they were to be fruitful and multiply (Gen 1:28), productive (Gen 2:15), govern their environment (Gen 1:26), and enjoy a food supply that went way beyond meeting just their needs (Gen 1:29). They were placed in a garden, not a wilderness (Gen 2:15), which was beautiful (Gen 3:6).

From the very beginning, God desired to bless his creation so that not only were their needs met, but they were able to accomplish his commands with full joy. He could have made the garden and his relationship with Adam and Eve functionally efficient without going to the trouble of making it an enjoyable place to serve God. The sheer awe-inspiring beauty of God's natural creation is breathtakingly and mesmerizingly beautiful. He could have made nature dirt brown or cloudy gray, but instead, he made it a kaleidoscope of color and shapes. These were given on top of the spiritual blessing of walking with God.

The conditionality of the prayer is uncomplicated. There is a promise with a condition. God will do something if we will do something first. We see the condition, "if you ask the Father for anything in my name," and then the promise, "He will give it to you." It is a simple sentence structure (as was the previous prayer). It is like when we tell our children, "If you clean your room, I will give you a Popsicle." Simple enough for a child to understand. There is a promise, and the recipient must meet the condition to receive the promise. It should be noted this is not a promise to fulfill every frivolous, self-serving, or sinful request. Still, we should not let that limitation distract from the actual immeasurable breadth of *anything* so that our cautions reduce the promise of anything to an almost nothing promise.

Contextually, this seems to include, at least, anything that relates to what they will need in the absence of Jesus to faithfully live for him and accomplish what he has called them to fulfill in their part of advancing the kingdom. This promise is wide-ranging when you think about all they would need every day. By application, it is equally as broad and comprehensive for us. It includes the myriad of things we need daily as we seek to live for him, be used of him in ways that please him, rear our children for him, make our homes godly refuges, live to be a witness through our life as well as speaking words of his greatness, love, salvation, and worthiness to be unconditionally worshiped. We also need to avoid being sidelined or physically destroyed by the wiles of the Devil before finishing our task. Add to this the thought of what particular individuals may require or benefit from. It would also include spiritual, emotional, relational, and psychological needs we might have or develop as we seek to follow him.

It is far-reaching into the coming days as well, extending to the end of our natural lives. But, God only promises to meet those needs if we ask. So, what if we do not ask? The answer is clear. The promise will not be realized, he will not meet those needs, and we will struggle and wander aimlessly and powerlessly. This understanding alone is enough to keep us praying all the time (Luke 18:1), lest we get to heaven and find out how much God wanted to do for and in us, but we did not ask.

John's words are not a prayer promise that is strictly limited to meeting our most rudimentary needs to live because of fear that we might experience joy from our prayers. On the contrary, one of the purposes Christ gave for praying is "so that your joy may be made full." We should not minimize that he ties Christian joy directly to whether we pray so he can answer our prayers. Christ desires to answer prayer and bless his people. How much joylessness do we experience because we failed to pray?

Interestingly, he is not telling us to pray for joy, although that is not wrong. This is not a prayer for joy, but it is about the joy he desires to give us when we make our requests known. These requests are not limited to requests *for* joy but are requests about many things so that our joy may be made full. There are countless conditionals in Scripture and an untold number of conditionals in the world, which should keep us praying lest we fail to glorify God and stifle the joy he wants to complete in us. God seems to answer generously rather than minimally.

James 1:5

God's wisdom is available to his people anytime we need it but on a conditional basis. There is nothing we do or think about that we do not need God's wisdom for guidance. Anyone who seeks to follow Christ knows this. If we are going to do anything, particularly if we are going to go to counseling or ask a friend for advice, we should first ask God for wisdom. If we are serious about following Christ, when we listen to someone preaching

Scripture, go to a counselor, or ask a friend, it is not really about seeking the wisdom of others; it is God's wisdom through them that we seek.

James says, "But if any of you lacks wisdom, let him ask of God, who gives to all generously and without reproach, and it will be given to him" (Jas 1:5). Accordingly, if we need wisdom about anything in our lives of serving God, like our relationship with a friend, family member, or spouse, or even how to raise our children, questions about our jobs, how to grow spiritually, pressing or upcoming decisions, or health and financial issues, the truth is this promise is for any decision and anytime we need wisdom, which is all the time. If you lack wisdom on any topic, ask God. Once we have prayed, God makes his wisdom known through a galaxy of ways such as experience, counselors, prayer, devotionals, Bible study, and preaching.

The word *ask* is a present-tense verb, which means we are continually or repetitively asking. Lord, I need wisdom because I'm going to talk to my boss, parents, a lost person, a friend about conflict, a doctor about possible treatments, ministry opportunities, or where to begin on a project, to name a few. Lord, I need wisdom about how to handle this money. Lord, I have this situation at work coming up, and I need wisdom. And God promises to give wisdom. But what happens if we don't ask? The condition that must be met for God to give wisdom is we must ask. If we do, he will give it; conversely, he will not give any wisdom if we do not. Therefore, if we do not ask, he does not provide wisdom for the task. Wisdom is available. He is ready to give it, but it is conditioned on our asking.

It is easy to see how conditional promises make no sense apart from libertarian freedom by which a person can choose to ask or not ask. If everything is determined to be what it is, or it does not matter if we ask or not because wisdom will still be given, it makes such conditional promises become nothing more than pointless gibberish. They even seem misleading. Conditionals only make sense if the promise is fulfilled when the condition is met and withheld when it is not, and a person can choose to do either. But if determinism is true, the one who asks is determined to do so, whereas the one who does not ask is determined not to ask. No determined person can experience the actual nature of a conditional, which is choosing to meet the condition and receive the promise or choosing not to meet the condition and not receiving the promise, and whatever the individual chooses, he could have chosen differently. But conditionals make perfect sense if we receive when we meet the condition of asking, and we do not receive when we do not meet the condition of asking. And we can actually choose to do either.

James 4:1–3

James adds even more clarity to the nature of prayer and the presence of libertarian free choice. He says, "What is the source of quarrels and conflicts among you? Is not the source your pleasures that wage war in your members?" (Jas 4:1). Resultantly, within us, there is a desire to please ourselves, to give ourselves selfish comfort, to avoid sacrifice, and that is where the conflict comes from. "You lust and do not have; so you commit murder. You are envious and cannot obtain; so you fight and quarrel." But notice that he concludes by saying, "You do not have because you do not ask" (Jas 4:2). The original word translated lust means strong desire. The context determines if the desire is evil or good; here, it is evil. The last line is illuminative, "You do not have because you do not ask." It neither says nor even suggests, in any sense, you do not have because I have not determined that for you, or you do not have because you are not smart enough, or you are not a man, or you are not a woman, or you are not old enough. No. It says you do not have because you do not ask. I do not know how it gets any more straightforward. God says you want these things, and you don't have them, so you get angry, sin, live selfishly, become bitter, and self-serving, but you do not ask the one who is your provider.

I do not want to go to heaven and find people I could have helped or learn about difficulties and even tragedies I could have avoided, or how I could have been used more of God but did not do so because I failed to ask. We may ask, not knowing if God has included what we are praying about as a conditional. But we can, it seems, rest assured there are some things we do not have because we did not ask.

When my daughters were young, there were things they wanted to have or do. At times, I would tell Gina, my wife, "Well, if they ask, I will do it for them." Maybe it was something they wanted to do but were afraid to ask, and I would tell myself if they ask, I will let them do it. My thinking was that if they did not ask, they did not want the object or opportunity that badly. Resultantly, I would think I will not concern myself with things they are not really concerned with.

Since my daughters are now both grown with children of their own, my handling of them as children has come up many times. They respond, you mean just because we did not ask you did not let us . . . or give us. . . . To which I reply, that's right. I am not sure whether I should feel this or not, but it is pretty enjoyable to hear them ask, "why not," "is that fair," or "how were we to know?" Then to watch them begin musing about things they remember they wanted or wanted to do and start asking me if what they are thinking about was one of those times. Yes, it is pretty funny. And oh yes, they definitely have some regrets.

Well, unlike me, God has told us we have not because we ask not, so ask! Just because people abuse the Scriptures we have mentioned to feed their narcissism should not lead us to unjustifiably temper our understanding of the breadth of these promises and deter us from asking. Understanding this promise affects our prayer life in areas we do not readily think about. For example, if someone pulls his car out in front of me, I want to pray for him rather than become angry and bitter. Sometimes, my initial response is not praying, but as I grow in Christ, I am decreasing the time-lapse from my initial response to prayer response. That is what I do because God may have brought him or her to mind for me to pray for them. I do not have if I do not ask. That is an explosively powerful statement. Add this to the truths that there are innumerable conditionals that God has given so that things will turn out differently if we pray than if we do not pray.

What if we ask and do not receive? James gives us one of the reasons our prayer requests go unanswered. He says, "You ask and do not receive, because you ask with wrong motives, so that you may spend it on your pleasures" (Jas 4:3). Simply put, they are defeated because they were walking in carnality. The same is often true of us. If you have asked and not received, this may be the problem. You have asked with the wrong motive so that you could feed the pleasures that are causing your carnality. We need to confess sin regularly (1 John 1:9) because answered prayer and carnality or sinful desires do not go together.

I can pray for someone's spiritual growth or for a couple's marriage to be strong, and I know these are in the will of God. But some situations are complicated, and we do not know if they are in God's will. But if we are walking with God and seeking to serve him, there is a great comfort for us when we pray. Paul says, "In the same way the Spirit also helps our weakness; for we do not know how to pray as we should, but the Spirit Himself intercedes for us with groaning too deep for words" (Rom 8:26). The Holy Spirit is working in our lives if we are walking in the Spirit, filled with the Spirit, and we don't grieve the Spirit. He helps us with our weaknesses. Part of our weakness is sometimes we don't know what to pray. Sometimes we just say, Lord, I don't know how to pray for this situation, or we pray what we are quite uncertain about. When we find ourselves in these situations, we can ask for the Holy Spirit's intercession for us. I will pray for what I know and trust the intercession of the Holy Spirit for the rest. I think the Spirit is helping us all the time, but sometimes the Spirit helps with communication that we cannot articulate.

This verse gives us great insight into the Trinity. "And He who searches the hearts knows what the mind of the Spirit is, because He intercedes for the saints according to the will of God" (Rom 8:27). God knows the mind of the Spirit, and the Spirit does not have to say a thing. That is the intimacy of the Trinity. Some people try to make Rom 8:26 about talking in tongues but notice it says too deep for words. And the word for "words" in the original is *alalētos*, which means "it cannot be uttered." The Holy Spirit intercedes with groans that cannot be put into words. It is nonverbal inter-Trinitarian communication. It is because God knows the Spirit, and the Spirit knows the mind of God (1 Cor 2:10–11). But it is a great comfort because sometimes we do not know all the circumstances. Or even how to pray about the outcome of an event. God may be using the event that we think needs to disappear to discipline, train, or prepare someone or even us. Thus, we securely rest in "Your will be done" and the intercession of the Holy Spirit, who is the comforter (John 14:6), without ignoring our responsibility to make our requests known to God.

Conditionals are not for God to say gotcha if we forget to mention something in our prayers. They are not to be understood as legal hurdles but rather relational promises. If we forget or miss something when we are seeking to pray as he has taught us, he may very well do more than we prayed for, as he often does because of grace and mercy. But, to ignore or minimize praying in the areas he has made conditionals as a part of our relationship with him is to miss the promise.

11

Praying in the Objective
and Subjective Will of God

ALL OF WHAT WE talk about, both conditionals and events that are determined, is included in what is called praying in the will of God (Eph 1:11; 1 John 5:14–15; 3:22). John says, "This is the confidence which we have before Him, that, if we ask anything according to His will, He hears us. And if we know that He hears us in whatever we ask, we know that we have the requests which we have asked from Him" (1 John 5:14–15). Now let me mention the context of this promise. In verses 1–5 of this chapter, John emphasizes that Christians are loved by God, love God, keep his commandments, love other believers, and overcome because we believe in Jesus. Verses 6–13 give evidence that Jesus in whom we have placed our faith is the true Savior, the Son of God. A form of the word testimony appears nine times in verses 6–13. The water (baptism), blood (cross), and the Holy Spirit speak in unison that Christ is the Son of God, the Savior of the world.

The concluding verse says, "These things I have written to you who believe in the name of the Son of God, so that you may know that you have eternal life" (1 John 5:13). That verse tells us why John provided evidence that Christ is the true Son of God. It is so that we who put our trust in him can know we have eternal life. Through John, God emphasizes not only is Jesus his Son and Savior of the world, but he also wants his people to know they have eternal life. It is not I hope I do type of salvation, but I know I do salvation. The inward testimony of this salvation is that when we have the Son, we know and cannot deny we have him, and with him is eternal life

(John 1:4). The inward witness of salvation cannot be proven to someone else, but neither can it be denied by the one who has the Son.

That brings us to the promise regarding prayer (vv. 14–15). John assures believers that our prayers are being answered in the same way he gives confidence that we can know Jesus is the Savior, and that we can be secure in our salvation. Therefore, he can say, "This is the confidence which we have before Him, that, if we ask anything according to His will, He hears us. And if we know that He hears us in whatever we ask, we know that we have the requests which we have asked from Him" (1 John 5:14–15). The promise he hears us (v. 14) is not just hear in the sense of being aware of what we are saying, but it is the idea of answering favorably (John 9:31; 11:41–42).

Accordingly, in the way we can know with absolute assurance we have eternal life (v. 13), we also can know he answers our prayers that are in his will (v. 15). Of this, there is no doubt. On several occasions, Jesus indicates that he or the Father will do whatever we ask if we ask it in his "name" (John 14:13–14; 15:16; 16:24, 26), keep his commandments (1 John 3:22), ask in faith (Mark 11:24), and abide in him (John 15:7). We are also told that our prayers must be in the power of the Holy Spirit (Eph 6:18; Jude 20). Prayer is the relational communing of believers with the Trinity.

God's promise about prayer is followed immediately by John's words concerning praying for an erring Christian brother or sister (v. 16). God promises to bring a sinning brother or sister back into fellowship so they do not die but live. But also notice the limitation. It is limited by a sin that leads to death. This sin could be so destructive that God needs to protect the church in an extraordinary way, as he did with Ananias and Sapphira (Acts 5:1–11). It could be referring to the unpardonable sin, which can be committed by a person who has just heard the gospel or by someone who is outwardly active in the church but not actually saved. The unpardonable sin is the final rejection of Christ with full illumination and revelation of the Holy Spirit, after which there is no possibility of repentance and faith (Matt 12:30–32; Heb 6:1–8; 10:26–27).

He does not forbid praying for someone who commits a sin unto death. He just says that is not whom he is talking about praying for. The ones he refers to are those sinning (present tense, which means continuous action). What we don't want to miss in this discussion is this. John just promised God hears our requests and answers them (vv. 14–15), and now he provides a great example that if we ask God to give life, bring a sinning brother into fellowship, he will. Of this, we can be assured. I do not always know the time, nor do I know if the sinning one is a brother or, as Paul mentions, "a so called-brother" (1 Cor 5:11). I do know that if I see a sinning brother, and he is not committing a sin worthy of immediate judgment, God desires to give him life and will give him life if we pray.

This verse is an example of how we can pray for other people, and God will work in their lives. Therefore, when we pray for the lost or the restoration of a Christian, we can know we are praying in the will of God. But when we come to God in prayer, we must come in faith. Jesus says in Mark 11:24, "Whatever you ask for in prayer, believe that you have received it, and it will be yours." Believe is a present tense and imperative mood verb. He commands the disciples, and us by application, to believe what we pray, that God is able and will do what we ask. We ask in his will, believing that we have our requests answered before we do. As Plummer notes regarding 1 John 5:14–15, "Our petitions are granted at once: the results of the granting are perceived in the future."[1]

Understanding this type of promise does not hinge on whether we are to pray according to his will in order to be answered because that seems to be a given. As I see it, why would we think that someone who did not desire to follow our Lord's commands, pray in the name of Jesus, and pray according to God's will should be granted an answer to his requests other than acceptance of his confession and repentance (1 John 1:9)? Instead, the question that must be asked to understand this promise is, what is the will of God? What is encompassed in God's will that would cause us to expect him to grant our requests? That question must be answered to understand this type of prayer promise and the place of conditionals in our prayers.

There are two aspects of God's will. One is his objective will, which is for everyone all the time. The Scripture is the objective will of God. It is the revealed will of God for everyone, everywhere, and everywhen. The second is the subjective will of God. While it is always in harmony with his objective will, it is God's personal will that concerns specifics related to the individual that is not explicitly covered in his objective will, Scripture. God's will for an individual is specific for that person and may not be precisely the same for anyone else, at least at a particular time and place. As Christians, we live our daily lives in recognition of both of these, evidenced by what and how we pray.

But most teaching or biblical commentaries about praying in the will of God are usually about the objective will of God. Other references on this

---

1. Plummer, *Epistles of St. John*, 121.

topic warn that the word "anything" does not give us carte blanche in our prayers. I agree with that caveat, but, unfortunately, I have been guilty of only making that warning or clarification and failing to explain what seems to be comprehended in praying in the will of God. My desire is to make more explicit what is meant by praying according to his will, which means we must understand what is included in his will.

Thus, are we to understand according to his will to include only events covered in his objective will, Scripture? Or does praying in God's will consist of both his objective will for all people and his subjective will for the individual praying? To clarify, praying in God's will would include the conditionals found in Scripture since those commands are contained in his objective will, and therefore, for everyone all the time. But would it also include conditionals that are a part of God's subjective will for the individual? I believe it does.

Those who believe everything is determined would, of course, only include what God has determined. This makes the whole concept of conditionals, whether in his objective or subjective will, seem rather pointless. Because the one who meets the predetermined condition was determined to do so (so there was never any doubt that the promise would happen in his life). The one determined not to meet the condition (so there was never any doubt that the promise would not happen in his life) has been eternally predestined, and nothing can alter that. There are no real conditionals.

But, as we have seen in Scripture and based on how we live our daily lives, there are conditionals. Meaning, God says he will do something that will make an outcome different if we meet his prescribed condition than it would be if we do not. In this case, God will answer our requests made according to his will if we ask and only if we ask. If we do not ask, he will not answer a non-request.

As an Extensivist, I believe praying in the will of God includes both his objective will for all and his subjective will for the individual, which would include the conditionals of both his objective and subjective will. I believe choice matters; our requests or lack thereof really matter in what happens. I think the conditionals of Scripture are just that. I believe praying in the will of God includes the conditionals of Scripture. Although the subjective will is seldom mentioned as being comprehended in praying in the will of God when we speak of the Scriptures that promise to grant our request, we do talk about and pray about countless things that are not explicit in God's objective will. All of this to ask, can God's will for us subjectively, personally, be a part of praying in God's will and with the promise he will give it to us if it is according to his will? If not, we should quit teaching people to pray about everything and even stop praying for God's will in our lives in a subjective way.

John says, "If we ask anything according to his will he hears us. . . . We know we have the requests which we have asked him" (John 5:14–15). Does that include only his objective will, or does it include his subjective will? If it includes his subjective will, and I think it does, then we can expect to find conditionals in God's subjective, specific, and personal will for us that are similar to the conditionals we see in his objective will for all people at all times. This understanding means I can pray for some things that are not explicit in Scripture regarding God's will for my life in the whole array of events that constitute my personal life in seeking to follow God.

I could be praying about a particular health issue in my family or a friend's family, knowing that God has comprehended such things in what it means to pray in the will of God. Some of which would be conditionals similar to those found in Scripture. I can know that some events will turn out differently if I pray than if I do not pray. We should view these prayers as consonant with his objective will, but we should not view them as a replacement for his objective will.

I could and should pray about health issues because it might be a conditional part of his subjective will to pray. But, I also must be aware that it may not, or the outcome I am seeking is not his desire for me. That is where I decide whether I trust him more than I trust myself. If so, the conclusion of our prayer, "Your will be done," is the prayer that extols God's objective and subjective will. God may be thinking of someone who needs the witness of Christ in a scenario that is best addressed if my health prayer is not answered. But it could simultaneously be his will that I prayed for what is a legitimate need since he said "in everything by prayer . . . let your requests be made known" (Phil 4:6). It would not have been his will if I did not make that known in prayer and just said, "Your will be done" because I would be skirting part of his objective will.

The request, "Your will be done" does not fit best at the beginning of our prayer as a replacement for making our requests known or as something that is necessarily contrary to our requests. Christ did place it first in what is traditionally known as the Lord's prayer (Matt 6:9–15), but he then made specific requests, which is surely fine. But, when he actually prayed in the garden of Gethsemane, he prayed his requests first (Matt 26:39). I am not speaking directly to whether you say it first or last, but rather that it cannot be used to bypass making our requests known, which saying it first is more likely to do. We have all heard people say, "Your will be done" at the beginning, followed by nothing. Consequently, practically speaking, it seems best at the close of the prayer because we recognize we do not know everything, and we trust him above everything. "Your will be done" involves the following. First, we desire God's will because it glorifies him and is best for us. Second, it is his will that we make our desires and requests known to him. Consequently, we are doing his will and praying according to his will when we make our requests known, and we are not when we do not make our requests known. Third, the nature of conditionals is that if we do not meet the required condition, it is his will that we miss out on the conditioned result.

For example, "Ask, and it will be given to you; seek, and you will find; knock, and it will be opened to you" (Matt 7:7). The very nature of conditionals is that if we don't ask, seek, and knock, God will not answer, give, and open the door so we can find. Therefore, his will includes making our requests known because what we pray about might be a conditional, which means that if we ask, it is his will to answer and change the outcome of the event we prayed about. Whereas if we do not ask, it is his will not to respond and change the outcome. Both to give blessing if we ask and withhold blessing if we do not are included in praying in his will. Therefore, if we pray "Your will be done" without making our requests known, we may very well be asking God not to answer our heartfelt but unasked requests.

Think about all the things we pray about daily, or I believe we should pray about, that fall into the category of the subjective will of God. We pray about health issues, job issues, where a person will go to school or college, money to build a church or pay a bill, providing or repairing a car, a need in a personal relationship, for children, for parents, marriages, time organization, safe travel, ad infinitum. If these things that are very personal, his subjective will, are not comprehended in Scriptures that speak of asking according to his will, then we should stop praying about them and teaching others to do so as well.

But, I believe that conditionals exist in both God's objective will and subjective will for the individual so that a person praying for everything in his life is praying in the will of God. People are in the will of God when they are making their requests known so long as they understand that God alone knows what requests are conditional. God does, in his will, provide what is needed to fulfill his subjective will for an individual as he does in his objective will for all. That is to say, I believe God answers prayer (Isa 37:15–21; Matt 7:7; John 16:23–24; 14:13–14; Jas 4:2; 5:16–18; 1 John 5:14–15). I believe his call to pray "at all times" (Eph 6:18), "without ceasing (1 Thess 5:17), "for all things" (Phil 4:6), means just that. We are always praying about everything, and my understanding of everything is that it means everything that is not contrary to God's nature and objective will.

For example, Debbie needs a car, so she prays specifically for God to provide her with a car. There is no Scripture to pray for a car except seeing it as covered under the command to pray for everything (Phil 4:6). Now when praying for a car, it could be that God does not want Debbie to have a car, or he could even want her to have a different vehicle at this time. It could be he never wants her to have one. That is possible, but it is also possible and seems highly probable that he wants Debbie to have a car.

God may desire Debbie to have a new car or used car, but it is a conditional. God has determined that area of Debbie's life is conditional. That is to say, if she asks, he will provide it, and if she does not ask, he will not. The pattern for conditionals in God's subjective will is the same as his objective will.

Therefore, it seems that praying about everything (Phil 4:6), all the time (1 Thess 5:17), includes God's subjective will as well. It actually would seem quite odd that it would not. That would mean there are not some things he desires for one person that he may not for another. And that he would not want us praying about those things that he wants to personally do in our lives, like a new job, where to live, and the countless things we do pray about regarding our families. But, that he does want us praying for everything in his subjective will for us fits well into praying all the time for all things.

Further, that we are to pray about everything in our lives tells us that not everything that rushes into our lives, be they opportunities or trials, is his will; to know, we have to pray. Finally, given that he has placed conditionals in our personal lives, we may assume they are similarly prevalent as we find in his objective will. These, as in Scripture, will come to pass differently if we pray than if we do not pray.

A person who senses God wants them to be a missionary will then pray about that, as well as such things as what country, when, through what sending organization, where to be trained, what to do specifically, and all the related familial and other ministry concerns. We know God does not call everyone to be a vocational missionary, and he does not call or desire all missionaries to go to the same country. Therefore, it seems undeniable that there is a subjective will of God in which we should make our requests known.

I remember well the process of accepting God's call to preach and then to pastor. This call is full of decisions that must be made to follow him step by step to the church where he desires you to pastor. The process for discerning these things is, to a significant degree, discovered through prayer. The application of prayer to discerning God's subjective will for each of us can be applied to seeking the will of God in a galaxy of possibilities. Many of which would probably be conditionals that will turn out differently if we pray than if we do not.

Unless there is an explicit Scripture or a clear overarching principle, we cannot know what things or events are determined by God and what is not until we have gone to him in prayer, and even then, we will not always know, nor do we need to know. All we have to know is that there are conditionals, and they will have a different outcome if we pray than if we do not. If we do not ask, we do not receive. It also seems that God's subjective will could include options. Namely, God could incorporate various options or details within a broader area of prayer that is conditional. He could have one particular option in which he includes multiple components that are conditional. If the person prays for all of them, God will grant all of them, but if he prays for only some, God will grant only some, provided they are conditionals.

For example, Bill is praying about where to go to school. There are three different schools Bill is considering. Bill prefers school A over B and C, but he is sure he does not want what he wants more than he wants God's choice. At the outset of thinking and praying about what school, Bill is unaware that God's choice is school B. He makes that known to Bill in the process of prayer, counsel, and thinking through various components of his decision. He may use persuasive leading and highlight option B through the Holy Spirit and even circumstances.

Bill understands, in God's subjective will for him, he may not want him to go A where his friends are going. By the nature of conditionals that he has established, we know that his will is not unconditional in every circumstance. The only things that are unalterable in a conditional are that if we do not ask, we do not receive and the range of options that have been set by God. Additionally, it may be within God's permissive will to permit Bill to go to any of the schools if Bill places his will above God's, even though what would be best for him is school B. Remember, we are never out of God's teaching range. He desires to teach us humility and the walk of faith within his desired will for our lives, but he can teach it even when we walk contrarily in what we think is best or even in rebellion.

God may condition his perfect will in a given situation on having made our heart known through our requests, and then with a great heart of trust saying, but Lord above all, I want your will. And his will was to give us what we specifically prayed for. But if we would not have prayed at all, or would have prayed and only said "Your will be done" without expressing our requests before speaking our trust in his will, he would not have answered our prayer according to his perfect will because that included making our specific request known. Reasons for this can be things like teaching the intimacy of prayer so he can better teach us the value of prayer, or so we can grow in our sense of walking in fellowship with him. To wit, he is not going to lead Bill to the school that would be best for him apart from specific honest prayer, much in the same way he is not going to give him the wisdom or peace he desires for him or us to have without first meeting the appropriate conditions of asking, trusting, seeking, and knocking.

But his perfect will, where Bill will be most blessed, is school B. That perfect will is known to Bill by praying and trusting it is God's will to pray through the options and be more desirous than anything that he ends up in God's perfect will. But it may go still further, what if what God wills for Bill also includes that B has financing, which is not available at school A or C. And that the money available with B is not automatic, but Bill must ask for it as well. What if included in his will were other conditionals like housing or the curriculum that he wanted Bill to take as opposed to what he would allow him to take in his permissive will. Friends he might meet or other opportunities that he might have while in school that are conditional, which means he will not have them if he does not ask.

In many scenarios, there could be so many possible conditionals that we could not think of all of them at one time. Consequently, we could not sit down and write a list of all the possible conditionals to pray for simply because we could not think of all of them at one time. We may just take them for granted if we do not really grasp the nature of conditionals. That raises the question of how we cover all the various components. One way is that we should pray about them as they come to mind. God has a plan for each one of us. In this scenario, if Bill prays and trusts the leading of the Holy Spirit, he will experience the best God has for him. In addition to these big decisions, there are many associated components that God has made conditional. God's permissive will lets us choose our desires instead of his best, but God will still teach us and accomplish his will in our lives.

The recognition of conditionals in both his objective and subjective will means that praying in the will of God is not something that is static or will happen regardless of whether we pray, ask, or seek; the will of God does not entail that all outcomes are determined. Instead, God's will, at least in the area of conditionals, includes our praying and making our specific requests known, without which, we are not praying in the will of God. That is because praying in the will of God includes seeking whether our specific request is the will of God or not. That includes the need to keep in mind that without asking, praying about everything, which would involve bringing our requests to him in prayer, we cannot truly be praying in the will of God. The reason we know this is that we know it is his will that we pray about everything. "Your will be done" is not a shortcut to praying in the will of God. When we pray "Your will be done" in place of making our requests known, it contains an element of insincerity since it is evident that we do not desire his will to be done in our lives, or else we would be doing his will by making our requests to him in prayers. Don't let "Your will be done" become a substitute for continuous praying about everything because God is not impressed (Phil 4:6).

Praying in the will of God includes conditionals, which means that if we do not pray about them, we are not praying in the will of God. One can see how the very nature of conditionals deepens one's walk and fellowship and trust in God. When Christ was in the garden of Gethsemane, he prayed, "My Father, if it is possible, let this cup pass from Me; yet not as I will, but as You will" (Matt 26:39). The first part of that prayer was equally the will of God (making his specific requests known), as when he said, "But as You will." As a servant who is totally dependent on the Father, he should make all his requests known and desire God's long-term best, whether it was according to his specific request or another path determined by the Father.

Accordingly, we all agree we are to pray in the will of God, and he gives everything according to his will. However, we have seen that our normal recitation of "Your will be done" does not answer the nagging question of what is comprehended in his will, which leaves unanswered what does it mean to pray in the will of God. We know some things for sure. It is his will that everyone be saved (John 3:17; 1 Tim 2:4; Titus 2:11; 2 Pet 3:9). That is static, absolute, and unchanging. We can know that all the time with every person. But we can also know that the conditionals of Scripture are just that. If we meet the condition he sets forth, he will grant the promise of the condition; conversely, if we do not, he will not grant the promise that is dependent on fulfilling the conditional.

Simply put, the recitation, "Your will be done," is not the totality of what is included in praying in the will of God. We make our requests known by praying in faith and the power of the Holy Spirit, and then rest in trusting God's will may be what we prayed or not, but we want his best. Accordingly, asking, even if what we ask for turns out not to be what he desires for us, is praying in the will of God, as was the case with Jesus in Gethsemane.

On the subject of salvation, Paul says, "That if you confess with your mouth Jesus as Lord, and believe in your heart that God raised Him from the dead, you will be saved" (Rom 10:9). There is a condition and a conditional promise. If a person will confess . . . and believe . . . he will be saved. So, what if he does not believe? Well, if the statement is genuinely conditional, he will not be saved. Thus, God's perfect will is that a person who confesses Christ gets saved, and equally his will, those who do not believe, do not get saved. The condition matters.

We find that God's will comprehends his desire for the salvation of all persons, which he wills to happen or not happen based on whether or not they confess Christ. Both outcomes are comprehended in the objective will of God. Similarly, in the subjective will of God, it can be within God's perfect will for a person to go to school B and be blessed in many ways, but that can be equally conditioned on whether the person asks or makes school B a request, including all the associated components of school B that God has made conditional. Spurgeon said, "Brethren, if there be a God, and if this Book be his Word, if God be true, prayer must be answered; and let us on our knees go to the sacred engagement as to a work of real efficacy."[2]

There is a pervasive urgency throughout Scripture to pray. There could be things that come to mind that we should pray for, but if we wait too long, it becomes the past, and the prayer cannot affect what it might have had we prayed when first prompted by the Holy Spirit. Understanding the presence of conditionals as seen throughout Scripture highlights the practicality of the numerous commands and calls to "pray without ceasing"

2. Spurgeon, "Praying and Waiting," 607.

(1 Thess 5:17), for "everything" (Phil 4:6), "with all perseverance and petition for all the saints" (Eph 6:18), and makes them even more relevant. Without this understanding, the commands seem to be only for the most dedicated prayer warriors, but in light of innumerable conditionals, they are seen for what they are. They are for the average Christian as much as they are for the most dedicated; they are essential for experiencing God and his best for us in this life.

In praying for specific things, we should not stop praying more generally or even for a group. I believe in praying specifically, and yes, I believe in calling someone's name in prayer. I also believe in group praying, like lifting up all the missionaries around the world that I do not know and will not know until I get to heaven. This type of praying is precisely what Jesus did when he prayed for the salvation of the world, "that they may all be one; even as You, Father, are in Me and I in You, that they also may be in Us, so that the world may believe that You sent Me" (John 17:21).

Resultantly, pray about everything. You do not have to think about what to pray about if you pray about what you think about. You will be amazed at how you will constantly be praying, particularly if you pray about every complaint or problem that you mention in your self-talk or to others. Saying I hope an event turns out well does nothing to affect the event. Worrying about the event does nothing to affect the event. Telling another person about a concern may make you feel better having shared it, although apart from seeking counsel and following biblical counsel, it does nothing to affect the event. But, making our requests known to God through prayer may very well change many outcomes. Therefore, by all means, talk to other people about your concerns, but only as a complement to talking to God and never as a substitute.

12

We Must Believe as If
We Have Received to Receive

Mark 11:22–24

JESUS CALLED THE DISCIPLES to faith in God through him for salvation, serving, and advancing his kingdom rather than Judaism. He called them to lives of robust faith (Mark 11:22–24). They would need faith to serve Christ when he was with them, during and after the crucifixion, and after the fall of Jerusalem to Rome in 70 AD, which would be a profoundly discouraging time to most Jews in the early church. In Jewish culture, having the holy temple in the holy city was inextricably bound to serving God. To see it destroyed meant they would need monumental direction and encouragement that they and the kingdom would continue to thrive, and so he assured them that faith in God would be enough.

"And Jesus answered saying to them, 'Have faith in God. Truly I say to you, whoever says to this mountain, "Be taken up and cast into the sea," and does not doubt in his heart, but believes that what he says is going to happen, it will be granted him'" (Mark 11:22–23). I do not believe the mountain to be merely hyperbolic. I understand this to be a literal mountain with metaphorical applications. Moving an actual mountain by faith transforms an impossibility for man into a possibility because of his faith in God who can do the impossible (Mark 10:24–27).

The point is, if they or his future followers need that mountain removed to do what God called them to do, it can be moved by God. Further, not only is the Creator capable of rearranging his creation, he is willing to do so if a literal mountain actually needs to be moved to advance the kingdom. He would move it in response to faith. Thus, the resources needed to serve God are not diminished by the absence of the temple, Jerusalem, or the whole nation of Israel when we have faith. Rather, it is the lack of faith that hinders our service to God (Heb 11:6).

However, to limit "mountain" to just moving physical mountains would impose far more limitation on the passage than I think is warranted. If there ever has been or will be a point in which God needs to move a physical mountain for the spread of the gospel, it would be so rare to make the promise have painfully little real-life application. Consequently, I think it has a metaphorical application; see Zech 4:7 for an example.[1]

To understand it literally with the metaphorical application would include physical mountains as well as a host of other needs, difficulties, and problems believers face. Such that could prohibit, severely hinder, or even make it more difficult than God wants it to be for that person at that time in carrying out the objective and subjective will of God, even if they are humanly impossible to handle. These situations are impossible from a human perspective, but with God, even things that seem impossible are possible. This understanding is the contextual backdrop for v. 24, which begins with the word "Therefore." This means, based on what Jesus had said and what they had seen, the following is the proper understanding and result. Jesus said, "Therefore I say to you, all things for which you pray and ask, believe that you have received them, and they will be granted you" (Mark 11:24). This promise is generally approached in one of three ways.

One: Some Christians approach it as a promise to grant anything and everything we ask when we believe, claim, and act as though we already have what we asked for, often known as "name it and claim it." They view it as a virtually unlimited promise. Because of the wording of the promise, one is within his right as a Christian to put God in a box, or some would say God put himself in the box, so to speak, which means that God *must* grant this type of request regardless of what the request is because we believe we have received it. They emphasize that he included "all things" so long as one believes and claims he has it as though he does have. Anything other than what is overtly sinful would generally be included. Commenting on this passage, Kenneth Hagin says, "Anything God has provided for you is a free gift you can receive right now. You don't have to wait. . . . Because healing

---

1. "A mountain is sometimes a symbol of difficulty. The fall of Jerusalem was a difficulty for the church as well as the synagogue." Brooks, *Mark*, 183.

is also a free gift from God, you can receive healing right now."[2] Joel Osteen says, "At the start of each new day, remind yourself: 'I am talented. I am creative. I am greatly favored by God. I am equipped. I am well able. I will see my dreams come to pass.'"[3] This Scripture is often cited as biblical grounds for claiming we can create our own reality. I think this perspective errs.

Two: Some Christians approach it more deterministically, although the deterministic emphasis is often difficult to detect. This view would caution that it is not a universal promise that includes every desire a person might have, along with presenting a determinative and static view of the will of God. You have to look closely to detect the determinism. Here are a couple of examples of this perspective.[4] R. Alan Cole comments, "We cannot pray in faith for anything that we like. In this matter, Jesus was '*thinking God's thoughts after him*' and willing his Father's will. That sort of prayer, if asked in faith, will always be answered, for it is *praying that God's will may be done* (as Jesus prayed in Gethsemane)"[5] (italics added). First, note the caveat that "all things" does not include anything we like, a limitation with which I agree.

But the caveat only tells us what is excluded; it fails to tell us what is included. It seems that we should be able to glean at least a few included things from such a stunning promise that God will grant "all things." But his wording that "Jesus was 'thinking God's thoughts,'" and that the sort of prayer Jesus was talking about is the one that "is praying that God's will may be done" can easily leave his comment without anything to pray for or request other than "Your will be done." Requests beyond praying for God's static or determined will to be done mean little or nothing. Such seems to reduce "all things" that we might request to one static, determined, valid request; "Your will be done." I agree that we should pray in the will of God, but I do not believe that reduces our prayers to what I think they are reduced to by his words.

John D. Grassmick says, "Jesus made this promise on the recognized premise that petitions must be in harmony with God's will (cf. 14:36; Matt.

---

2. Hagin, "Faith Brings Results!," paras. 14–15. See also *The Agony of Deceit* edited by Michael Horton and *Christianity in Crisis* by Hank Hanegraaff for more on misdirected creative faith.

3. Osteen, *Become a Better You*, 22–23.

4. My intention is not to superimpose determinism on Cole and Grassmick's comments, but simply to explain how they are reflective of and consistent with determinism. Both are Calvinist commentaries.

5. Cole, "Mark," 968.

6:9–10; John 14:13–14; 15:7; 16:23–24; 1 John 5:14–15). *This enables faith to receive the answers God gives*"[6] (italics added). Here again, we find the warning not to take "all things" to mean all things without limits, and I certainly agree. But notice he contends that Jesus made the promise based on the petitions being in harmony with God's will. The purpose of being in harmony is so that the petitioner will have the "faith to receive the answers God gives."

In other words, we learn that "all things" does not mean all things, but we do not learn what things it might include, other than enablement for petitioners to "receive the answers God gives." Please reread the promise because, to me, it seems to be saying much more than merely what is necessary to receive God's will. Notice the determinative implication of these words. It seems to reduce our part to pray in preparation for being open to receive what God has predetermined he is going to do; therefore, it seems equivalent to praying "Your will be done" without any need to make our requests known.

This deterministic implication raises the question of just what are we supposed to believe we have received before God grants it? It does not appear to be our requests, as the verse says, unless we request what is already God's determined will. But if God's will is a static singularity that is determined, it seems like we are going to accept and obtain that anyway. Grassmick seems to reduce praying and believing our requests to be nothing more than a mechanism to mold us so that we will receive what we are going to inevitably accept anyway since God works everything according to his will (Eph 1:11).

---

6. Grassmick, "Mark," 158–59. See also William Hendriksen's comment; "The dramatic figure, in the light of its context, which speaks of faith and prayer, must mean, therefore, that no task in harmony with God's will is impossible to be performed by those who believe and do not doubt. . . . We should not try in any way whatever to minimize the force of this saying and to subtract from its meaning." I appreciate his acknowledgment that "no task in harmony with God's will is impossible" if we believe and do not doubt, but I think he still fails to clearly indicate that some things are conditional so that our prayers change some outcomes from what they would be if we did not pray. Hendriksen continues, "It should be borne in mind that such praying and asking must, of course, be in harmony with the characteristics of true prayer which Jesus reveals elsewhere; in fact, it must be in line with all of scriptural teaching." Hendriksen and Kistemaker, *Mark*, 459–61. He then provides the essentials of praying in the will of God; however, his words, again, give the caveat, with which I agree, but seem to lack a clear indication that "anything" refers to conditionals, or if there are true conditionals; more precisely, if we pray, it is the will of God to answer, and if we do not, it is his will to withhold. Therefore, his will is not static.

But if everything is determined, is God not going to do his will any-way, even if we are not prepared through praying and believing? In the end, it seems we are left with a command to believe we have received "Your will be done" as if we have already received this inevitable outcome. If we are determined, or in a deterministic system such as Calvinism, that actually takes little faith. At least, within Calvinism, there seems to be a lack of a clear explanation of how there are true conditionals (as this very verse demonstrates), wherein it is God's will to grant some requests if we ask that will not be granted if we do not ask, thereby changing outcomes.

Well-known Calvinist pastor and commentator John MacArthur said, "Prayer is not an attempt to get God to agree with you or provide for your selfish desires, but that it is both an affirmation of His sovereignty, righteousness, and majesty and an exercise to conform your desires and purposes to His will and Glory."[7] While I agree prayer is not to provide for our selfish desires (Jas 4:3), and prayer affirms God's character, his explana-tion grants no room for conditionals, which are clearly in Scripture and this passage. Further, his statement makes prayer only a determined vehicle to conform us to God's determined will. We have seen already, which is confirmed repeatedly throughout Scripture, praying the conditionals of Scripture is God's will and do bring him glory (John 14:13). This emphasis on determinism is consistent with Calvinism, although Calvinists often speak inconsistently with Calvinism's compatible moral freedom as though prayer and choice can change some outcomes. That is to say, they frequently talk like man has libertarian freedom (conditionals really are conditionals), which Calvinism in doctrine utterly rejects.

A conditional statement is a statement or command with a stated or implied corresponding dependent outcome. In the case we are studying, it pertains to prayer. God says if you ask, I will answer. Further, condi-tionals commonly portray people as being able to act or refrain. Concern-ing prayer, this means that his people can ask or not ask, and their choice determines the outcome. Therefore, some present or future results will be different because we pray than if we do not. None of this reflects the true micro-determinism of Calvinism; they use the same words but mean a very different thing. Prayer may be a part of the determined process to get to the determined outcome, but no one can actually choose to ask or not ask unless they were determined to do so; therefore, their actions do not and cannot change the predetermined outcome.

7. MacArthur, "Prayer Is Not an Attempt."

The thing determinism promises to be given (God's will) if we pray and believe is precisely the same thing we are going to receive if we do not pray and believe. I do believe God works all according to his will (Eph 1:11), but it is the absolutely static and predetermined presentation of his will that I do not believe is thoroughly biblical because such a view reduces conditionals, like the one in this verse, to non-conditionals. As previously stated, a conditional is a statement or command with a stated or implied corresponding dependent outcome. The outcome is based on the person meeting the condition, which the person can choose to meet or choose not to meet. If you ask (condition), I will give this to you (action). The outcome is certain if we meet the condition; if the condition is unmet, God withholds the promise. That is the will of God.

In the verse we are considering, the condition is "All things for which you pray and ask, believe that you have received them," and the outcome or promise is, "and they will be granted you" (v. 24). Therefore, if you meet God's condition, he will grant your request, but if you do not, he will not, which does not seem to be true if our request is reduced to "Your will be done." I am not suggesting that we are to pray outside the will of God, or that God is doing something outside of his will, but, instead, that God's will includes real conditionals. As such, if we ask believing, he will grant them because that is his will, or if we do not ask believing, it is equally his will not to grant them. Expanding "all things" so broadly that we can create our own reality seems to make God's will conform to our will, whereas the determinist's language seems to reduce the conditional promise to grant "all things" to a non-conditional "Your will be done."

Three: Other Christians approach it from the perspective of what I might call cautiously expansive. There is more emphasis on the place of faith and the true nature of conditionals in prayer without the recognizable determinism. James A. Brooks comments on vv. 23–24, saying, "The faith Mark seems to have had in mind is not that which is needed to work spectacular miracles but to accomplish the Christian mission. . . . The statement is not to be universalized and applied without exception, but neither is it to be localized and confined to the original disciples or ignored as having no practical value. Faith is an indispensable element in answer to prayer."[8] He includes the needed caveat against overstating the promise, but he also gives a broad practical purpose for the promise "to accomplish the Christian mission." He further clarifies that the promise is not limited to

8. Brooks, *Mark*, 182–83.

the apostles but includes all of us endeavoring to follow Christ faithfully. I agree with what Brooks has presented, but I would like to expand on his insight so we can begin to see the full weight and application of the promise given the nature of conditionals.[9]

Conditionals are commands or statements that include a promised action if the condition is met. This verse fits that definition. Christ conditions it generally on praying and asking, but specifically on our belief that we have received what we ask for before we receive it. Of course, this conditional promise would need to be in the will of God. The real question is not whether we are to pray according to the will of God, but what has God comprehended in his will? What do we mean by the will of God? Is God's will static and determined, or does the will of God include conditionals within his permissive will? It seems to include determined events as well as conditionals, as we have seen throughout the Scripture. We see God's permissive will, in which we find conditionals when we see him permitting people to do what is undeniably against his best for them or when he grants something because they asked.[10]

Conditionals in Scripture tell us that it is insufficient only to pray "Your will be done" because how does believing we received it for God to grant it have any real meaning if we only pray "Your will be done?" In accordance with the nature of conditionals, we are to pray about all things (Phil 4:6) believing we received them, which meets the condition of the promise given. All things seem to include all things in Scripture (God's objective will for all) and his specific will for each individual that is not explicitly mentioned in Scripture (God's subjective will for the individual). His personal or subjective will would include such things as personal ministries, jobs, health, marriages, dating, education, childrearing, where to live and go to church, and personal planning about one's day. God's subjective will for the individual is not in contradiction to his objective will or in place of it, but, instead, it is in addition to it. It is personal. For example, God commands

---

9. My expansion on his comments is not to imply my take would be his, but only to say his language suggests an even broader application than we might first think.

10. While Calvinism speaks of God's permissive will, it lacks any essential difference from his decretive will, which includes man being endowed with compatible moral freedom; consequently, God's permissive will is no less determined than everything else in man's world. Whereas, true conditionals actually result in a different outcome if we pray than if we do not pray, and since man is endowed with libertarian moral freedom, he can actually choose to pray or not to pray.

everyone to pray (objective will), but he does not lead everyone to live in the same neighborhood or go to the same mission field (subjective will).

The question we leave to God is whether he has made what we are asking for conditional or not. Mark 11:24 is definitely conditional; if we ask believing as though we have already received it, God grants it. If we ask without believing as though we have received it, he does not grant it. But the uncertainty lies in whether or not what we specifically ask for (within his subjective will for us) is conditional or not. Our humility in prayer emanates from the fact that we do not know everything God may have determined or made to be conditional. Thus, praying as though we have received is not something that grants us demand status, cornering of God, or a magical formula. It is the confidence we will receive what we ask for if we believe we have received it provided God designed what we are praying about to be conditional. Conversely, given the nature of biblical conditionals, we know that if we fail to ask for something he has made a conditional, it is his will to withhold from us what he would have granted if we had asked.

Another requirement God places on receiving our prayer requests is "whatever we ask we receive from Him because we keep His commandments and do the things that are pleasing in His sight" (1 John 3:22). One of his commandments is to forgive (Mark 11:25–26), without which we cannot receive his answer to our prayers (Matt 6:14). God grants requests of those who love him as evidenced by keeping his commandments (John 14:15) and freely choose to do things that are pleasing in his sight such as spontaneous acts of worship, praise, thanksgiving, serving, and a heart to glorify him in even the most mundane things (1 Cor 10:31).[11] This interpretation highlights the relational nature of salvation and prayer.

Consequently, I believe when we combine praying in light of conditionals, believing we have received what we ask before God grants it, and praying within his will, which includes his permissive will, we can pray believing God will answer our prayer, provided the event we are praying about was established by him to be conditional. While I can know the conditionals that are recorded in Scripture, I cannot know with the same assurance all the others that may exist. In other words, I can know all the

---

11. Other things mentioned with regard to answered prayer include a humble and sincere heart and mind (Matt 6:5–6), not doubting (Jas 1:6), perseverance (Matt 7:7; Luke 18:1–18), desiring the will of God (Mark 14:36; 1 John 5:14), walking according to his word (1 John 5:1–3), asking in Christ's name (John 16:23), and married men treating our wives as joint heirs (1 Pet 3:7).

conditionals of his objective will (Scripture for all people all the time), but I cannot know what they are according to his subjective will (what he desires to do in an individual's life). Therefore, I can know this verse (Mark 11:24) is conditional, but I cannot know whether the specific request I am making in applying this promise is conditional or not unless it is delineated in Scripture.

A believing prayer of a devoted follower of Christ as commanded in our verse might sound something like this; at least it would include a heart reflective of these ideas. Lord, without any doubt, I believe right now, before I see the result of my prayer that if you have made the event I am praying about conditional, you will grant my request. I believe I receive that answer before I can see or demonstrate it. But God, I know that only you know whether you have made the event on my heart and lips a conditional. Therefore, I close my prayer of believing requests with "Your will be done."

Notice that kind of heart and prayer includes all the components of God's plan for praying. We pray as one who desires to honor him with our heart and life (1 John 3:22), we make all our requests known (Mark 11:24; Phil 4:6), believing we have received what we ask for before we receive it (Mark 11:24), leaving whether our request is a conditional or not with God (1 John 5:14), and rightly closing with "Your will be done" (Matt 26:42).

Observe the place of "Your will be done." If it comes first in our prayers, we will be more likely to ignore the other components that God taught and commanded—just mentioned in the preceding paragraph. But coming last means that if God made and included in his will that our request is conditional, he will grant our request because we asked. But, if we pray "Your will be done" first, without making our requests known, we may very well be asking him not to grant our heartfelt but unspoken request because while, with conditionals, his will is to grant our believing request, it is also his will to withhold things he knows we want but did not believingly request.

Two final thoughts are; first, these components are not legalist steps, but rather they are relational. They flow from the new life Christ has given us and are, therefore, not a legalistic burden to us, but rather a way to experience God more consistently and powerfully (1 John 5:3). Prayer is at its core a relational practice between God and his followers. Second, it seems that one sure implication of this promise is that we should not worry about what we prayed about once we have prayed believing. We can continue praying about it in accordance with the biblical emphasis upon persisting in prayer (Matt 7:7; Luke 11:5–10; 18:1–18), but that is quite different from worrying about what we have prayed for in faith because if it is designed by God to be conditional, he will answer.

I was working on this book while in Oxford, England, in the summer of 2019. On Monday, July 29, Gina, my wife, and I drank coffee at Café Nero, a daily routine. As we entered, I saved a table for us by putting my windbreaker on the chair and my sunglasses on the table. With our table never leaving my sight, I went to help Gina get our order. We then received our order and went back to our table, and set the tray down on the table where I had left my sunglasses. We did not notice they were not there until we were ready to leave.

When we gathered our things to leave, we realized my sunglasses were gone. We scoured our sitting area, and everywhere I had gone while in the café, my sunglasses were not to be found. I determined that someone stole them while I was in line and apparently glanced away from our table. I was greatly discouraged because they were prescription sunglasses, which meant I would have to spend our remaining week in Oxford without them, go to the doctor when I arrived home, and spend a few hundred dollars on replacing them. Also, I could not believe someone had actually stolen them and that I naively was so trusting or careless. We searched everywhere and asked the baristas if they had seen them or had they been turned in; they said no. They said if my sunglasses turn up, they will keep them for us. Our search for them included me getting on my hands and knees to search for them all to no avail. Eventually leaving the café, walking a short distance, and then returning in utter disbelief to look again (yes, some say I am a little obsessive).

I sought to process my disappointment, naivety, and carelessness in prayer for the rest of the day. The next morning, I did the same. Basically, I prayed as I have described above. I asked God to work so that I could have my sunglasses back; although God already knew how important that was to me, as a part of our relationship, I spoke the strength of my desire to him. I told him I was sorry for my neglect, and that I believed I would get them back according to your word if this prayer request concerns something you made a conditional which only you, my Lord, can know. Maybe, it is not. Perhaps you are going to do something in me that returning them would stifle. I have made my believing request known, and in everything, I praise you and fully trust what you will do in this situation, "Your will be done." Knowing that his will may have included this situation as a conditional, and I would get my sunglasses back, or it may not have.

The next day, I wrote the very section of the book which you just read, and then we made our daily pilgrimage to Café Nero. All morning, against my feelings that I would never see the sunglasses again, I kept repeating my believing prayer. Knowing that it may not be conditional, I also sought to praise God that this event was not serious; all things considered, and unlike many, I would be able to replace my prescription sunglasses with another pair. As we arrived, I saved the table, and Gina stood in line. This time I did not leave anything at the table but me—as Gina has lovingly said to me, you don't have to be dumb all your life. I heard the baristas talking with Gina, and then she said, they found your sunglasses. There are other details, but that they found them was the significant end of this prayer adventure. The most dramatic moment was when they handed them to me, and the barista said, "I found them at the table where you were sitting."

I do not know what happened to the sunglasses, nor how they got where he said he found them, nor do I need to know. However, I can definitely say that *beyond a doubt, I know* they were not at our table when we left, and I now have them. Gina and I would testify to both. We spent well over one and a half hours reflecting on this prayer event. Further, I do not think the sunglasses turning up missing while I was writing this book on the day before I wrote this section and were returned the next afternoon after I finished this section was a coincidence.

Those of you reading this may think I am a sensationalist or embellisher, but those who know me best would say the very opposite. The reality is, I greatly struggle with praying in this manner, in part because of my analytical personality. Although I undoubtedly cannot prove it, I do think God did this in this way to speak to me personally about the work I was doing in this book. The event offers no proof that what I am writing is reflective of the Scripture; only Scripture can do that. It did have an intensely encouraging, relational, and spiritual impact upon Gina and me, which is a significant reason for God putting conditionals in the Scripture in the first place.

In the scheme of eternal issues, advancing the kingdom, this event is less than insignificant. Although losing my glasses was quite upsetting to me, I did understand that while personally meaningful, whether I got them back would not stop the kingdom from advancing or Gina and me serving God. It is similar to God knowing the number of hairs on every person's head (Matt 10:30); that clearly seems to be an insignificant kingdom issue. But, God knows that because he is God. What God did for me, although eternally insignificant, was relationally and personally meaningful. I think God does many of these things when we follow him because, well, those are just the kinds of things God does at times just because he is God and loves us, even caring about the little things.

I include this one last word on this practice of praying while believing. It was not only difficult for me to do so in this circumstance, but it continues to be something on which I have to work. I can say this experience has now, over two years later, proven to help me spiritually in my practice of believing I have received before I see the evidence without committing the sin of those who take this to the extreme. As I said, it surely includes not worrying about the request for which we are believing him. It may include more, but at least that.

13

We Need to Pray for Ourselves

Matthew 5:13–16

IF WE WANT TO influence other people, we need to pray for ourselves first because our life, for good or bad, affects those around us. We often refer to our life influence of others as our testimony. We want others to see Christ in us because that means we are walking in the commands of Christ, and those commands are not a burden (1 John 5:3). Because it is not our life we want them to see, it is Christ's life being lived in and through us (Gal 2:20). If you're going to pray for your child, spouse, boss, or a friend at school, start with yourself. God can use your testimony in others' lives, particularly the ones for whom you are praying (Phil 2:15; Titus 2:8; 1 Pet 2:12, 15; 3:16).

No one is won to Christ by seeing someone live a Christlike life without also hearing the truth. But if we don't live the Christian life, what we say will have little credibility. They may not even want to listen to us. Speaking to his disciples, Jesus said,

> You are the salt of the earth; but if the salt has become tasteless, how can it be made salty again? It is no longer good for anything, except to be thrown out and trampled under foot by men. You are the light of the world. A city set on a hill cannot be hidden; nor does anyone light a lamp and put it under a basket, but on the lampstand, and it gives light to all who are in the house. Let your light shine before men in such a way that they may see your good works, and glorify your Father who is in heaven. (Matt 5:13–16)

If salt is contaminated or loses its saltiness, it no longer serves its purpose.

Similarly, we are the salt of the earth (testimony of Christ to the world), but if we become contaminated by the ways, cares, aspirations, and morals of the world, we are no good to the work of the kingdom. Our good works are the light of our redeemed life by the light of the world (John 8:12). Our light is to shine so others can see it, but if our light is hidden by sin, we fail to shine.

The Bible does teach an eschatological (future) glorification of God. In the final judgment, all people, whether saved or damned, will glorify God because he is righteous and gracious. But the primary way God receives glory now is by a person becoming a believer by faith in Christ and then reflecting the light of Christ to the world. We are commanded to let our light shine, and if we want to influence other people's lives for the kingdom, we need to let our light shine. Therefore, it may be wise to pray for ourselves before we pray for those we seek to influence for Christ. We might pray, Lord, protect my words. God, protect me from my temper. God, protect me from saying things that will hurt people unnecessarily. God, protect me from misrepresenting you. God, help me to have godly behavior. God, may my words only reflect my unity with you before a lost world so that the world may believe. Praying that our lives truly reflect Christ in every way should keep us pretty busy in prayer. There are people we want to influence, but we begin by praying for ourselves, so the reality of our lives matches the words that we speak.

God may have someone come live in your home. You didn't expect it. It may be inconvenient, and it inevitably changes everything for your family and you. But God wants them to see authentic Christianity, up close and personal. You will need to pray for them, but because of the difficulties, loss of privacy, and constant demands, you will need much prayer for your spouse and you. We need not pray that our children see us as perfect, but, instead, that they see us handle our failures by confessing our sins to God and one another. If our children see us as parents mishandling a problem, we need to go to God in confession, then go to our spouse, and then go to our children. Tell your children what you did wrong and that you confessed it to God, your spouse, and now you are asking for their forgiveness. Let them experience Christ in us lived out. Resultantly, they will glorify God because they saw our good work, which is the life of Christ in us and through us.

Titus 2:1–11

This passage in Titus reminds us of the importance of praying for ourselves and other Christians so that we live lives reflective of the unity we have with the triune God. Paul gives instructions about how pastors, older women, older men, servants, younger women, and younger men are supposed to live their lives. Paul relates two reasons directly to God and one to the Christian. He says the reasons for his instructions are so that "God will not be dishonored" (v. 5) and "so that they will adorn the doctrine of God our Savior in every respect" (v. 10). Regarding the Christians' testimony, Paul says, "so that the opponent will be put to shame, having nothing bad to say about us" (v. 8). The first mention is to young women when he says, "To be sensible, pure, workers at home, kind, being subject to their own husbands, so that the word of God will not be dishonored" (Titus 2:5). It's all about living a life that honors the word of God and having a Christ-honoring testimony in and through the home.

He says to the younger men, "In all things show yourself to be an example of good deeds, with purity in doctrine, dignified, sound in speech which is beyond reproach, so that the opponent will be put to shame, having nothing bad to say about us" (Titus 2:7–8). These guidelines speak specifically to the purpose of living right, and these instructions are so that our lives lived before detractors give them nothing bad to say about us. It is difficult to overcome the confusion left by people who claim to be Christians, but they do not live the Christian life. When you are trying to win people to Christ and influence them for the kingdom, it is very difficult when they have a host of Christ-dishonoring images of carnal Christians to overcome.

Our conduct is not only honoring or dishonoring to God, but it is also what people consider when they form an opinion about God and Christianity. Some may say it does not matter what people think, to which I say, where did you get that? Does it matter what your children think? Does it matter what your spouse thinks? Of course, it matters. It is not the most important thing in the world, but it does matter. Above all, it matters what God thinks about us, but God also thinks it matters what people think about us because he wants people to come to him. He loves the world and wants all people saved. God says it does matter what your neighbor thinks of you. It does matter what your boss thinks of you. If you are a slave, it does matter what your master thinks of you. God's reasoning is because he loves them and wants them to be saved. He commands Christians to live salty lives so people will be saved through our words and lives that give credibility to our words, and by that, he will be glorified before the eyes of men (Matt 5:16).

Paul then says, "Urge bondslaves to be subject to their own masters in everything, to be well-pleasing, not argumentative, not pilfering, but showing all good faith so that they will adorn the doctrine of God our Savior in every respect" (Titus 2:9–10).[1] He is basically saying, tell slaves to be honest. When they are told to do something, do it. Do not argue. It is easy to see how we can apply this in our present-day to employer and employee relations. When your boss asks you to do something, just say OK. Do not start arguing about it or try to second guess him. You are not the boss.

What's more important? You getting to express your undesired opinion or representing Christ, which might lead to your boss or employee getting saved? To adorn the doctrine of God means that in all respects, they will make our Savior attractive. So that all who watch them, their masters, fellow slaves, and others, will see the Savior and be attracted to him. Is that not astonishing? That our life can make someone desire to follow the one we follow? It is by our behavior that others see our testimony that we adorn the doctrine of God.

Do you know why we need to pray that our life, our testimony, reflects Christ to the world? Do you know why God is concerned about Jesus being attractive to people? Here is Paul's answer, "For the grace of God has appeared, bringing salvation to all men" (Titus 2:11). That is why God is concerned. God wants all men to be saved. God has done everything from a provisional standpoint, and he is continually working to see people saved. He is even working in us, so when we walk in his word, he uses our testimony to reveal the attractiveness of Christ to draw people to salvation.

Nothing is given here about a list of dos and don'ts, but just living for God. God loves the people we are around, and a significant influence on people coming to know Christ is through the testimony of our lives. Part of our testimony is what we say and how we say it, and part of it is how we conduct ourselves daily. How we conduct ourselves when we handle difficult circumstances such as when someone treats us wrongly, we are taken advantage of, someone wrongfully takes what is ours, or how we respond to people slandering us will exert a substantial influence on others. Our response should please God, but he is not the only one watching. The eyes of our children, friends, coworkers, extended family, and neighbors are all

---

1. This passage is not addressing whether slavery is right or wrong, but only the need to live honoring to Christ in whatever state we are in.

on us, and that matters to God and should matter to us. How will we be-have? How will we respond? Like never before, the average Christian can be heard and seen by the world on the internet and social media. We must be as diligent about what we say and do in those venues as we are in our own neighborhood.

When rearing our children, we intentionally sought to raise them ac-cording to Scripture and incline them to love Christ. However, one of the great lessons we learned from our children when they became adults was how significantly they noticed things we did just because we were trying to follow Christ without realizing we were influencing them at all. The things to which I refer were not done so they would see us doing them or even with the intent of influencing them. Rather, we were doing them to help us follow Christ, but they benefited by watching what we watched or listening to what we listened to or said to others. Children are watching and listening as you make decisions and figure things out, and that is influencing them toward or away from Christ. They not only see and hear what you see and hear by using various forms of media, but they see where your heart is, and that has the eternal potential of inspiring them toward God.

Living the life of a witness is motivated by one thing, and that is love. It's a love for God and a love for what God loves. And God loves people to be saved. God has bought and brought salvation to all mankind. We may and should be concerned about our children being saved. But no matter how great our concern is, it is a fraction of God's concern, comparatively speaking. He paid a much greater price. He's working every day through his salvation plan, our life, and in them. This love flows out of our unity with the Trinity (John 17:20–21). It flows through us when we walk in that unity of truth, love, purpose, and will.

What happens if someone at work gets promoted over you, and let's say the promotion is rightfully yours? What is more important than the promotion is how you handle not getting it if we are talking about eternal issues. People will know you should have received the promotion, and how you handle that can have eternal consequences. We hear testimony after tes-timony of how people were affected by someone like a nurse, grandmother, or a coworker, and this is one of the passages that specifically teaches what they are talking about. Do not ever wonder why you are concerned about how others view your life. It's because you love God, and you love what he loves, which is to see people being saved. This concern will undoubtedly require us to pray for others and pray in the moment, but we should surely pray for our testimony before and during such events so that our lives may make Christ attractive to the lost.

1 Peter 2:11–12

Internally, spiritual warfare is our fallen humanity (our flesh) waging war against the new us (our spirit) created in Christ as a new creation (2 Cor 5:17; Eph 4:22–24). The theater of battle for most spiritual warfare is in the mind. Even if your emotions are tossing to and fro, the battleground is in the mind. Accordingly, Rom 12:2 and Eph 4:23 remind us to renew our minds; the present tense means we are to be constantly renewing our minds. We renew our minds by learning the Scripture, praying in fellowship with God, and living out the word. But spiritual warfare and renewing our minds are not all about you or me. Peter says, "Beloved, I urge you as aliens and strangers to abstain from fleshly lusts which wage war against the soul. Keep your behavior excellent among the Gentiles, so that in the thing in which they slander you as evildoers, they may because of your good deeds, as they observe them, glorify God in the day of visitation" (1 Pet 2:11–12).

Spiritual warfare is the enemy seeking to dishonor God through us, to make us representatives of God in which people will not see Christ as attractive and be saved. Christians are often unjustifiably ashamed because they really have to struggle in an area that is not pleasing to God. They say, at times, I feel like giving up. Actually, I am glad when I hear someone say they struggle because the Bible says we struggle as Peter just did. Paul says, "For our struggle is not against flesh and blood, but against the rulers, against the powers, against the world forces of this darkness, against the spiritual forces of wickedness in the heavenly places" (Eph 6:12). Satan and his hellish force will exploit our weakness and attack us in the area he thinks he can be most successful. Our flesh will seek to gratify ungodly desires and even desires given by God but satisfied in an ungodly way. It is when someone says she does not struggle with anything that is the problem. The struggle is to be expected, or we will not put on the armor of God (Eph 6:11, 13). We will not pray intensely to avoid some struggles and have the spiritual strength to win others.

The day of visitation referenced in 1 Pet 2:12 refers to Christ's second coming. Some believe it refers to the time he will look on the wicked in judgment. But the second coming is not only about judgment, but the conquering of evil and looking on those who are his people, the saved. God will be glorified even by the wicked on that day because it will highlight his holiness and righteousness. But that does not seem to be the point of Peter's words. He says the reason for keeping our behavior excellent is "so that . . . they may because of your good deeds, as they observe them, glorify God in the day of visitation."

It is the wicked seeing our behavior that makes Jesus attractive that results in their glorifying God, referring to those who will be saved. We are to fight the spiritual war in this present hour because we are to glorify God in everything, and our good works glorify him (1 Cor 10:31; Eph 2:10). Our fight is so that he may be glorified by those who come to Christ in part by his people living godly lives before them (Matt 5:16). Luke tells us, "Simeon has related how God first concerned Himself about taking from among the Gentiles a people for His name" (Acts 15:14). God is glorified when his people are united with the Trinity in love, holiness, purpose, and will. Other than God, the major theme of Scripture is the plan of salvation that he brought to all men (Titus 2:11). We should prioritize the same.

At times, the early Christians were called atheists because they did not practice Caesar worship. They were called cannibals because it was said they ate human flesh and drank human blood, in reference to the Lord's Supper (Matt 26:26–28). Peter is saying the best antidote to mischaracter-izations of Christ is when critics get to know you and intimately observe your life, and your life refutes all the slanderous things they have heard or said about Christianity. Then they see our Savior as attractive. We pray for them and us so that we may live lives that lead them to be attracted to our Savior and, by God's grace, get saved and shout hallelujah with the rest of his redeemed in heaven in the day of visitation.

Almost everyone's testimony includes the influence of someone or maybe several Christians' lives. While many later told the person how their lives influenced them to follow Christ, quite often, some who had the great-est influence never knew they did. They were influenced by a person they knew for a time that later moved away or transferred to another job or a family member who died before they told them. I remember hearing a man share his testimony and mentioning how he walked by his grandmother's room one night and saw her kneeling in prayer. He said God used that event to start a work in his life. He did not know what she was praying for, and he never talked to her about it, but something began to change in him. Some of the people I worked with on the railroad were dedicated

Christians, and their lives not only played a role in my salvation in 1978 but even strengthened me to be a witness for Christ after I became a Christian. And their influence is as fresh on my mind as ever. If you have the opportunity, tell those who made Christ attractive to you, thank you!

It seems safe to assume unless we live a hermitlike life, others are watching how we live. Someone may be watching your life over many years, and your only interaction may be antagonism or questioning of your faith. But they are watching your behavior. And God is empowering your behavior to work in their hearts eternally. So, the concern I am expressing regarding praying about our own testimony is not to be reduced to a mechanical list of dos and don'ts. It is about loving God and loving those whom God loves that are watching us. This knowledge inspires us to live to give a clear example of Christ to influence them to desire to know more about him and prayerfully to know him in salvation. It is astounding to think that God works so we can live lives that dispel slander, stereotypes, caricatures, and hatred for Christ and transform those resentments into a love for Christ. This kind of life takes prayer, the kind of prayer that is unshakably convinced from Scripture that God does some things when we pray that he does not do when we do not pray.

Many who are hostile to Christianity in America were hurt in the past, which is the source of their animosity. Gina and I were giving out Bibles when we were poor college students in Dallas. When we ran out of our own Bibles to give away, we went to our church to ask if they would give us Bibles to give to people to whom we were witnessing. The church discussed our request in the monthly business meeting. Because we were young, we made the mistake of bringing one of the persons who wanted a Bible to the meeting. While many of our church members were supportive, one deacon stood up and said, "I don't think we should be giving Bibles to people who are not members of our church. That's not good stewardship. So I recommend that we give Bibles to people when they walk the aisle and join the church." When the meeting was over, we had no Bibles to give out on visitation. Sadly, this young girl looked at us and said, "I wouldn't take a Bible from this church for anything." And in tears, she walked away.

God will bring people in close, and it is there that they will see the real us, especially children. But don't think that you cannot lose your temper, or you have to be perfect, or others can't see your mistakes. You will be utterly defeated if that is the case. But they do need to see that following Christ is more important than anything else.

I remember when I was offered whatever financial assistance I needed by a university vice-president to send my oldest daughter to that university. Between the time of telling my daughter and her becoming all excited and ready to go, the university made a decision that I thought was a serious breach of trust with the convention of which the university and I were a part. I knew I would have to speak out publicly against the action of the university. Because I was going to speak against them, I did not think it was right for me to benefit financially from them.

Consequently, I wrote to the vice president expressing my deepest gratitude for his and the university's kind generosity toward us. I also said that I would be speaking against the action they took, and because I would speak out against them, I could not take the money. I then told my daughter that she would not be able to attend there because I could not afford it without the help I was offered. I still clearly remember our emotional talk at the kitchen table. We both cried while discussing the change. She was deeply disappointed and saddened. I remember the hurt she experienced, realizing she would not attend the school closest to our home and where her friends were attending. I remember how deeply it hurt me to see that I had so disappointed her. She ended up going to college in another state.

Sometimes, keeping our integrity with God and before others is not easy. It can be excruciatingly painful. This again reminds us that we need to pray for others, especially our children, but we need to pray for ourselves so that we will make the right choices in the moment of testing. When Gina and I hear our grown children talking, we wonder how they do not remember all the times we messed up. My answer is God just graciously covers it with the blood of Christ, so they remember our faith in Christ they saw in our strengths and even in our weaknesses. They saw the faith in our lives when we asked for their forgiveness when we acted wrongly. What tempers the impact of our failures on them is their eyewitness account of knowing that following Christ overshadows everything else for us, even during our many failures. I believe that commitment to follow Christ is shown by our love for God in following him and our love for the people he salvifically loves because he wants them saved. This kind of life cannot be lived without prayer for ourselves.

Much of the necessity of prayer is due to God's establishment of conditionals. God permits a certain amount of options that are available or changeable by prayer. So that a person who does not pray, say for a loved one who is sick, may, when all the facts are known, learn that God would have intervened had he prayed. Conversely, the one who does pray will learn in heaven how many outcomes were different because he prayed. Our prayers that change the way things turn out are not such that they change God's will, but instead, they are comprehended by God in his will, which we refer to as his permissive will. God's perfect will is what is best for us, but God permits us to make choices that are not his best for us. For example, choosing to pray is pleasing to God and best for us, but he allows us to choose not to pray.

It is essential to keep in mind that even though some things will be different if we pray, not everything we pray about will be different. We could have a child still go down the wrong path despite our most earnest and untiring prayers. That is not because prayer is not effective, but instead that it was not a conditional. When I was a young pastor, I believed if you preached the word and you prayed, God would protect, and Satan could not get a foothold in the local church. That belief was from my naïveté rather than the Scripture. The Bible did not promise that. On spending considerable time alone with God, he reminded me about the garden of Eden. That was the perfect environment created by the perfect God, and yet Satan got a foothold. I then realized that my beliefs were not consistent with Scripture. Therefore, we should not think we can pray enough to stop everything or control everything. Man's freedom, and therefore, his choice, matters.

Our Lord Jesus made his request known to the Father in the Garden of Gethsemane. He prayed, "Father, if You are willing, remove this cup from Me; yet not My will, but Yours be done" (Luke 22:42). It was the will of God that Jesus made a request to avoid suffering the wrath of God for our sins, but it was not the will of the Father to grant that request. When Christ made his request, he knew it was the will of God for him to do so. He modeled what he has taught us to do (John 14:13; Phil 4:6). He also knew it might not be the Father's will to grant his request, and so he submitted to the Father's will for him.

This example is the nature of known and unknown conditionals—those not explicitly taught in Scripture. Some things we know are conditional promises—if we ask, he grants, and if we do not ask, he does not grant his promise (John 14:13–14). Others, as illustrated in Christ's prayer, we do not know if they are conditional or determined by God, but we should ask. Importantly, God did not give Jesus his request, but he did desire his only begotten Son to make the desire of his heart known to him, just as he taught his disciples, including us, to do. Whether it is Christ or us making our requests known to God, it is not to inform him, but rather it is relational. God desires we make our requests known, knowing he has made some things to be conditioned on our asking, because talking with him and experiencing him is crucial to our relationship with him. Our relationship also includes trusting God for the outcome when what we prayed for is not a conditional. We must learn to trust like Christ, *yet not My will, but Yours be done*. God's will for Christ would be exceedingly more tormenting than what Christ had prayed for, but God did not forsake him. He ministered to him in that hour by sending angels to care for him. I believe he will also minister to us if we trust him as our Lord did (Luke 22:43).

I close this chapter with the following necessary insights regarding conditional outcomes. One, God alone knows what he has determined to be conditional and what he has determined to be unconditional. Two, we can know the ones the Scripture is explicit about, which is his objective will for everyone, and humbly pray about those that may be implied or arrived at by application. Three, the conditionals that are available for a given person or circumstance, God's subjective will for the person, are determined by God's sovereign choice and not because of the will or choice of libertarian free beings. There is no formula for humans to create them. God determines what are and what are not conditionals as well as the range of options for each person.

Additionally, there may at times be, and probably is, an expiration date, so to speak, when God has deemed a prayer about a conditional to be effective. In some circumstances, this is easy to see. For example, we could wait too long to pray for the job we wanted. We waited to pray until the job had already been given to someone else and is now a part of history so that it is now *scientifically* impossible to get the job since that would require changing history, which is *scientifically* impossible,[2] backward causation.[3] Therefore, we should pray about what we think about when we think about it!

---

2. Although God could intervene and override the natural order of time (Josh 10:1–14; Judg 7:17, 36–40; Isa 38:8), in the normal course of time, barring such a supernatural intervention, backward causation does not happen. Without a miraculous intervention of God, backward causation is impossible.

3. This is not to discount a situation in which the person who got the job might quit or be fired, and the job become available again.

14

Eight Biblical Examples of Praying for Other People

PRAYING FOR OTHER PEOPLE is a common practice in Scripture and our daily lives. We are either praying for someone or asking others to pray for us. But we seldom pause to ask just how exactly does that work? We have emphasized that Christians believe in two mutually exclusive views of free will. If compatibilism is true, how can we meaningfully pray for others? Prayer cannot change outcomes in people's lives if everything is determined. Even the inclination to pray for someone or ask them to pray for us is determined. The determinist is left with saying God determines the means to the end and the end. But that does not help because the one who does not pray or is not affected by our prayer is determined not to pray or be affected by prayer, and the one who prays for them is determined to do so, which even includes the words prayed. The one who prays and the one who does not pray are both doing precisely what God determined for them to do.

Additionally, I have never met anyone who asks for prayer in a way that indicated they believed their request was going to happen even if they or someone did not pray—determined. That is to say, they are just doing what God determined them to do. No. They believe they need prayer, and prayer changes some things to turn out differently than if prayer was not offered to God. They need help, and prayer provides God's help that would not happen if they or someone did not pray.

How does praying for someone with libertarian free will work? I can choose to pray for them, but can one person change another person's free will? Can one person pray for something to happen in another person's life that the person does not want to happen? Parents pray for their children all the time; we pray for their protection, to mind us better, the friends they choose, for their salvation, and a galaxy of other things. But, just how does that work? Do they not have free will?

We must keep two things in mind when praying for others. First, we can pray for God to use our prayers to influence other people. However, we cannot pray for things to cause a person with libertarian freedom to decide a certain way, and he still be held responsible for that particular decision. For example, we could pray for various things that God might do to influence the person for whom we pray to be saved. These influences can be strong, even life or death strong, but the exercise of faith in Christ can be caused only by the person, or else it is not a free decision for which he is responsible. Even humans can override another person's free will. For example, when a person wills to drive fifty mph in a forty-mph speed limit zone and a policeman pulls him over and tickets him, he is responsible for the decisions that led to being pulled over. But, being pulled over was not a freewill decision because it was forced on him by the policeman, even though the choices that led to being pulled over were freewill decisions. The policeman made the free choice to pull him over.

As we have also seen, the Bible teaches that some things are determined by God apart from human influence. While God can override libertarian freedom when he chooses, that does not mean man becomes determined in all of his decisions. Generally, when we are praying for other people, we are praying that God will work circumstantially, influentially, or persuasively in their life so that the person may be led or influenced to make the right choice, thereby remaining responsible for the decision. With libertarian freedom, you can be strongly influenced without being forced or caused. A person with libertarian freedom, who has the choice to do right or wrong, can never be guaranteed always to choose right. You can persuade and lead, but there are no guarantees. Persuasion is not coercion. They still can choose to act or refrain.

What do we mean when we pray for God to break a person, meaning break their rebellion and sin? If by that we mean work as strongly as possible, given the way God chose to create man, that is OK If we mean to break in a causal way, that would generally be contrary to how God chose to make man; although, as we have seen, God can and does override man's freedom at times.

Second, when we want to affect other people's lives, what we pray must be according to or consistent with the revealed will of God. If we pray something, to which the Bible clearly speaks, like someone's salvation, improving a marriage, not getting a divorce, our children loving God, or say the protection of our children from danger, then we know our prayers are consistent with the Scripture. If we pray in areas that the Bible doesn't speak to specifically, we need to pray consistently with the principles found in Scripture.

We can see many examples of parents praying for God to work persuasively and protectively on behalf of their children. Parents regularly pray for God to work in the lives of their children in such ways as bring them to salvation, protect them, work in correcting their attitudes, or provide good friendships. Whether God works persuasively or even causally is up to him. If your child is getting ready to marry someone who is an abuser, as a parent, you would quite expectantly pray for their protection. You would pray with everything in you that God would stop that marriage or bring the abuser to repentance. God may work persuasively in your child's life to call off the wedding. It is even possible that he may override their free will, but that is his decision.

The following leads us to pray passionately and biblically. One, recognizing that God does some things in many areas when we pray that he will not do if we do not pray. He may very well change the outcome to be different from what it would be if we would not have sought his help. Two, God is God, and he will always be God. Therefore, we pray knowing God changes some things through prayer, but only he knows which things he will change and how he will change them. As I have said, given that God created man with otherwise choice, which entails the ability to do wrong when that option is available, we must recognize that God has designed the universe so that many good and many bad things will happen because of the choice of humans. But we know "God causes all things to work together for good to those who love God, to those who are called according to His purpose" (Rom 8:28). Some difficult things that have happened to a person may be made good in this life, but all will be made good in the life to come for believers.

We know from Scripture that we can pray for our child's physical and spiritual protection because, as parents, we are our child's protectors, humanly speaking, and they do not always know what is best. We prayed for our daughters' friendships and their dating relationships, not to mention everything else under the sun. We prayed that one day they would marry godly men who would love God, them, their coming children as well as lead their family to follow God. But we have to stay vigilant as Peter warns, "Be of sober spirit, be on the alert. Your adversary, the devil, prowls around like a roaring lion, seeking someone to devour" (1 Pet 5:8). We are praying consistently with Scripture when we pray for the spiritual and physical protection of our children. Scripture never says you cannot pray to protect or even pray against an enemy that wants to hurt somebody you love. It does say pray for our enemies, but we are to protect those within our watch care as well (Exod 22:2).

Jesus said, "If you ask Me anything in My name, I will do it" (John 14:14). This instruction includes praying for kingdom advancement, which consists of praying for God to work in people's lives as our Lord Jesus did (Luke 22:31–32; John 17:9, 20–21). Hudson Taylor (1832–1905) is a well-known missionary to China who founded the Inland China Mission. He believed John 14:13 and sought to live it, and it became woven into the fabric of his life. It says, "Whatever you ask in My name, that will I do, so that the Father may be glorified in the Son" (John 14:13). Writing about the life of Hudson Taylor, Eugene Myers Harrison said, "In China he would have to depend utterly on his Lord for protection, supplies—everything. Lest a dismal failure befall him later on, he determined to test thoroughly the Saviour's promise: 'Whatsoever ye shall ask in my name, that I will do.' He resolved to learn, as he said, 'before leaving England, to move man, through God, by prayer alone.'"[1]

Rather than depending on man to change himself or men to change men, Taylor depended on God to change people. He waited on God to move men, change them, change their decisions, and change their lives through prayer alone. Is it possible? Sometimes we hear something like that and say "amen." But you have to remember that every person has libertarian freedom. We are talking about praying for another person to change. Now you have to put this in perspective. You say I like that. I'm for it. But that means someone else can pray and change you. And how does that fit with people having libertarian freedom? I believe what Hudson Taylor said, and I believe it is a compelling statement. Maybe you cannot witness to

---

1. Harrison, "J. Hudson Taylor," para 16.

someone, you are not even able to have contact with them, but God can and often does work when we cannot through prayer.

Luke 22:31–32

Scripture makes it clear we are to pray for others. In this passage, Jesus is praying for Peter. A straightforward reading of this event gives the distinct impression that Jesus thought his prayer for Peter would have an impact. I think Jesus believed prayer does affect outcomes, not everything, but some things. He is our advocate (1 John 2:1), which means he speaks to the Father on our behalf. That is what praying for others is all about. His advocacy was given to encourage John's readers when they failed God and sinned. That encouragement provides every indication that his intercession makes a difference in outcomes so that if he did not advocate, things would often turn out differently. To Peter, Jesus said, "Simon, Simon, behold, Satan has demanded permission to sift you like wheat; but I have prayed for you, that your faith may not fail; and you, when once you have turned again, strengthen your brothers" (Luke 22:31–32). The story of Satan demanding permission to sift or shake Peter brings to mind Job chapters 1 and 2.[2] Sifting like wheat is probably the idea of severely shaking with temptation (Amos 9:9). The word translated prayed is *deomai* in the original and means begged or pleaded. Jesus warns Peter that Satan will bring all hell against you, but I have been pleading for you. Jesus' prayer reminds us that we are to pray that we will not enter into temptation (Luke 22:40, 46), and we need others to pray for us as well.

Jesus' prayer is not some superficial prayer; this is a spiritual battle over the future of Peter and, to some degree, all the apostles. Jesus believed prayer played a role in Peter's coming through this battle with the devil. That is, his prayer could result in a different outcome than if he did not pray. The struggle is so intense that Jesus seems to believe Peter's faith could fail. And failure doesn't mean giving in; it means walking off. The Greek word translated "fail" is *eklipe*, and it means "to cease from an activity which has

---

2. The first pronoun, "you," is plural, which may indicate Jesus was thinking of Satan's desire to tempt all the disciples at various times in the coming days. The remaining times "you" appears in Luke 22:31–32, it is singular, indicating that Peter is the focus of this pericope; which is precisely what we see in the verses that follow.

gone on for some time . . . to stop, to forsake."[3] Jesus prayed for Peter not to succumb to Satan's hellish temptation to stop trusting and following Christ.

Then Jesus tells him that when he returns, he is to strengthen his brothers. Some believe this statement of Peter returning means that Christ knew he would not fail. In his deity, of course, he knew, but not in his humanity. I do not think the passage suggests that everything would work out, and his prayer, pleading for Peter's safety, did not really matter. It makes his begging seem rather theatrical if his prayers did not matter.

Instead, I believe he is practicing what he taught (Mark 11:24; John 14:13–14; John 16:23–24). He is doing exactly what he told the disciples and us to do when we have or see needs that need to be met for the kingdom to advance. He asked the Father in faith. Therefore, it seems that Jesus thought his prayer mattered in whether or not Peter returned in faith to lead the apostles. One thing seems quite sure; Jesus did not act like his choice to pray, nor the outcome was determined. If he did believe such, that would reduce his earnest begging the Father on Peter's behalf to being overly dramatic.

Even the idea that one human can strengthen another is a significant component of this whole idea of conditionals. If people are determined and cannot choose to be strengthened, how can Peter strengthen them? Why try to strengthen your brothers if everything is determined? Those determined to be strong will be. Those determined to be weak cannot be strengthened. A determinist might say that, like Jesus' prayer, Peter strengthening the others is a part of the process. But in a deterministic system, prayers are not substantially related to the outcome, for they as well as the outcome are determined.

To be substantially related would mean if the prayers were not there, the outcome might have been different, and the prayer could not have been there had the person chosen not to pray. In determinism, the determined prayer cannot be removed from the determined process, but if it could, hypothetically, the end result will still happen. The means to the end are only incidentally related. That is to say, God could have decided to use singing the Babylonian national anthem if he so chose because the prayers are just a determined cog in the determined machine. In contrast, I believe Scripture repeatedly shows us that prayers are substantially related to the outcome, which means that if they are not prayed in conditional situations

---

3. Louw and Nida, *Greek-English Lexicon*, 657.

(which can happen since libertarian free beings may choose not to pray), the outcome may be different.

By any normal reading of this passage, it sounds like the host of hell was really against Peter, and Jesus was praying Peter would not lose the war and walk away from God and everything God had called him to do. Jesus also prayed that after the encounter with Satan, the battle would leave him stronger than before, and he will use his life, strength, and experience to strengthen his brothers. In this prayer, we also see that he is praying about the present (the sifting) and the future (Peter will strengthen his brothers). We should be mindful when we are praying about a present need, to include related future needs if the request is met, or even so the present need will be met. As we see Christ doing with Peter, we are told to pray for one another as well (Jas 5:16).

John 17:15–21

Jesus prayed for others. This passage is a part of the high priestly prayer. He is interceding to the Father on behalf of the disciples. He prays, "I do not ask You to take them out of the world, but to keep them from the evil one" (John 17:15). Christ was interceding for the apostles because he knew they had a humanly impossible task before them. He continues his prayer,

> They are not of the world, even as I am not of the world. Sanctify them in the truth; Your word is truth. As You sent Me into the world, I also have sent them into the world. For their sakes I sanctify Myself, that they themselves also may be sanctified in truth. I do not ask on behalf of these alone, but for those also who believe in Me through their word; that they may all be one; even as You, Father, are in Me and I in You, that they also may be in Us, so that the world may believe that You sent Me. (John 17:16–21)

Christ prayed for the apostles who believed in him, and he prayed for all who would believe through the word of the apostles, which includes everyone saved after his prayer for the apostles. But he goes even further. He prays that the apostles and all those who believe after them may be one. The oneness he prays for is rooted and patterned after the Trinity's oneness, but it is not identical. It includes unity in truth, holiness, will, purpose, and love, but it is more than that.

As believers, we are spiritually united to the Trinity. But Christ's prayer seems to be directed at more than that. He prays that the unity believers have with the Trinity, we also will have with each other. He prays his followers will be unified in his love and holiness, around his word as truth, and in commitment to his will; while not exhaustive of his prayer for oneness, his emphasis in these verses is on world evangelism. He prays for this unity "so that the world may believe that You sent Me" (v. 21). He prays for the same world of humanity that is lost (Rom 3:10–18), that he loved and came to save (John 3:16) and died to take away their sins (John 1:29) and draws by grace to salvation (John 12:32). He prayed for all of us who are believers as well as the world of humanity around us so that they might believe. When we pray for a lost person to be saved, we are praying like Jesus. When we pray for each other, we are praying like Jesus.

Also, he does not pray for organizational unity in verse 21 but organic unity. The purpose of the unity is, speaking of believers, "that they may be in us," followed by the purpose of that kind of oneness, "so that the world may believe that You sent Me." Imagine you have an unbelieving family member, and whether they like it or not, when they are around you, they see a difference between you and them and others who are not Christians. Then they work with someone who demonstrates a unified testimony of the presence of Christ in their life and the difference that makes. Then at their child's soccer games, that same presence and difference are evident in the Christian parents there. You see, that is the unity of presence, difference, and spirit that is difficult to ignore. He gives a further purpose of the oneness, saying, "I in them and You in Me, that they may be perfected in unity . . . so that the world may know that You sent Me, and loved them, even as You have loved Me" (John 17:23). Jesus also wants the world to know that God loves his followers, and the presence of God's love can be seen in and through his followers' lives. This unity is a testimony to the world of what it means to become a follower of Christ.

Romans 9:1–3; 10:1

Paul prayed for the salvation of the Jews. "Brethren, my heart's desire and my prayer to God for them is for their salvation" (Rom 10:1). As Jesus prayed for the salvation of the lost world, Paul prayed for the salvation of the Jews that he loves. You can see the passion Paul has in his heart and prayer for these people when he says, "I am telling the truth in Christ, I am not lying, my conscience testifies with me in the Holy Spirit, that I have great sorrow and unceasing grief in my heart. For I could wish that I myself were accursed, separated from Christ for the sake of my brethren, my kinsmen according to the flesh" (Rom 9:1–3). What passion he has for the salvation of others. Paul knows he cannot exchange himself for the salvation of others. He is the preeminent theologian of the New Testament. But his heart is to give it all up if they could know Christ is the long-awaited Messiah sent by God. I am always humbled by Jesus and Paul's love for the lost. There is much room for growth in my passion for the lost.

But if God has inviolably and unconditionally elected some to salvation who cannot miss being saved and damned the non-elect so that no possibility exists for them to be saved (as Calvinism teaches), why did Jesus (who would have developed that plan if it exists) and Paul (who wrote half the New Testament) pray so passionately for all to be saved? Their prayers' passion and scope go well beyond just being a part of an eternally determined process.

If God the Father developed the plan to damn the non-elect because it pleased him, he had no mercy or compassion for them. If unconditional election is true, where did Jesus and Paul get their salvific compassion for everyone who is lost? It could not have come from the Father because he developed the plan to withhold compassion from the non-elect lost. Did Jesus go against the Father's non-compassionate stance against the non-elect lost in loving, and praying for them to know him, thereby showing compassion on them? From whence did it come? Where did Paul get his salvific compassion because it surely did not come from the Father if unconditional election is true? Am I to believe Paul has more salvific love and compassion than the Father? No! He is expressing the salvific love for all, which comes from the Trinity.

2 Corinthians 13:7

Paul prayed for the Corinthians' moral integrity, "Now we pray to God that you do no wrong; not that we ourselves may appear approved, but that you may do what is right, even though we may appear unapproved" (2 Cor 13:7). Paul is praying for other people, and in this case, it is the Corinthians. But can he know it is the will of God that they do no wrong? The answer is yes. God does not want people doing wrong, sinning (1 Cor 12:20–21). Even though Paul is praying what is obviously God's will, he still has to check his motive for why he is praying for them to make good choices—"not that we ourselves may appear approved."

Paul wants them to do right, even if he may appear unapproved. Paul is OK not proving that Christ speaks through him. He does not mind if others do not approve of him; uppermost in his mind is the Corinthians' moral virtue before God. If that can be accomplished without an apostolic showdown with them, that would be good.

If the Corinthians are determined according to compatibilism, then if they follow their greatest desire and do wrong, that is expressly what God determined them to do. In that state of affairs, Paul was praying for them not to do wrong, but his desire to pray for them is also determined. Resultantly, Paul is determinately praying the Corinthians will not do what God predetermined them to do. Confusing indeed! The Calvinist might say, as we have seen before, God determines the means to the end as well as the end. But that does not help because that still requires that God determined the Corinthians' wrongdoing, and Paul did not pray out of deep love (at least an undetermined one that originated with him) because God determined that he pray.

It becomes like a masterful puppet show, with God pulling strings so that some people do the very thing he commands them not to do because he predetermined them to do it, which makes his stated desire for them to do right lack sincerity since in a determined state of affairs, if he wanted that, they would do it. Paul's prayers would be meaningless. Such a determined perspective does not make God seem more majestic and sovereign, but rather incapable of being sovereign over people with otherwise choice. Therefore, the libertarian view is not elevating man but rather the God who created man.

If Paul and the Corinthians have libertarian moral freedom, it all makes sense. Paul chose to live for God and knew it was God's will and desire for all his children to live morally (1 Pet 1:15–16). God has provisioned everything needed. The Corinthians were choosing to live contrary to what God desired and designed them to do. But, Paul knew God answers prayer. He also knew whether someone lived for God or not was conditional. It was conditioned on the person's choice, and libertarian free beings can choose to pray for God to work in their lives. And libertarian beings can choose whether to live for God or not. Thus, Paul persuaded (Acts 19:8; 28:23; 2 Cor 5:11) and prayed for people as he persuaded and prayed for the Corinthians.

2 Corinthians 13:9

Paul prayed for the Corinthians' spiritual maturity, saying, "For we rejoice when we ourselves are weak but you are strong; this we also pray for, that you be made complete" (2 Cor 13:9). Paul is content with being weak or being seen as weak because he had learned that when he is weak, he is strong in Christ (2 Cor 12:10). Here you have Paul praying quite specifically for the Corinthians. His prayer for them is that they are made complete. Complete is the Greek word *katartisin*. This noun is used only here in the New Testament. We most often see the verb form, *katartizō*, meaning to restore something (Matt 4:21; Gal 6:1), or make it useful for its purpose. It means to be put in order or make complete (1 Thess 3:10). Another form of the word is found in Eph 4:12 (*katartizmon*). It means to "prepare, equip, or mature."

It is related to the word in 2 Cor 13:11 *katartizesthe*, which says, "Finally, brethren, rejoice, be made complete, be comforted, be like-minded, live in peace; and the God of love and peace will be with you." "Complete" is the word *katartizesthe*. It is a second-person plural imperative, which means it is a command for all the Corinthians to obey. It can be translated in the middle or passive voice. In the passive voice, it would mean be restored. In the middle voice, it is the idea of mend your ways, make the changes yourself in order to be restored.

In either case, we see Paul's prayer is congruent with what he taught elsewhere and commanded by the authority of God. That is, it is the will of God that if they are incomplete, they are made complete—mature (v. 11). Whereas in v. 7, Paul prayed the negative that they do no wrong. Now he prays the positive that they are made complete. Meaning, go all the way to completion of what God wants you to be.

What we see in both prayers is this. First, the Corinthians are not what they should be. Second, they are not what they can be. Third, they are not what God desired or designed them to be through salvation. Fourth, prayer seems to play a significant role in bringing about change. Fifth, Paul prayed because he chose to pray, and the Corinthians' improvement will, in no small measure, depend on how they respond to Paul's prayer. This prayer only makes sense in a world where the Corinthians have libertarian freedom.

To read this from a deterministic perspective is to transform a passionate prayer into a prescribed recitation. It is to make the entire call to pray, obey, resist, and mature a symposium of contrarieties and bafflegab.

For this scenario to be transpiring in a compatibilist system of determinism is like the Rocky Mountains in obstetrical labor to produce a molehill.[4] What is the point? This perspective is why we can read compatible commentators who handle the passage as I am, libertarianly—even though doing so contradicts Calvinism and compatibilism.

It is impossible to meaningfully understand and communicate all the conditionals in Scripture from a compatibilist perspective; therefore, they speak libertarianly when they deal with them except for an occasional insertion of unconditional election or determinism, which is frequently not even suggested by the text. Nevertheless, their shift to speaking libertarianly when needed makes people think they are a milder Calvinist. When in reality, instead of making them a milder Calvinist, it makes them an inconsistent Calvinist. Compatibilism does not provide a biblically consistent reflection of Scriptures' prayers, commands, desires, gospel presentations, or calls to grow spiritually, obey God, and flee immortality.

Commenting on 2 Cor 13:11–14, David K. Lowery asks,

> Did the Corinthians respond positively to Paul's warning? Yes. Paul had conditioned the expansion of his ministry in other areas on the problems in Corinth being resolved (10:15–16). He followed the writing of this letter with a visit of three months during which time he wrote the letter to the Romans. In that letter he wrote, "Now . . . there is no more place for me to work in these regions" (Rom. 15:23). His appeal had been heeded. The Corinthians were now obedient.[5]

Consequently, it seems like they improved some, but whether they did or did not, you still have Paul praying for their change for the better, and by every regular reading of the passage, they could choose to follow his prayer in v. 9 and command in v. 11.

It is clear to the unbiased reader that Paul believed prayer could change outcomes, at least in situations we know as conditionals. Paul did not think that everything was determined. He is praying for particular things. Thus, the question to ask is this: if he didn't pray, would the outcome have been any different? If determinism is true, the outcome was determined, and so was his prayer. But one surely leaves reading Paul's words with the understanding that he prayed not because he was determined to pray, but, rather,

---

4. Based on Bergsma, *Speaking with Tongues*, 13, quoted in Smith, *Tongues in Biblical Perspective*, 114.

5. Lowery, "2 Corinthians," 585.

that he chose to pray for others, knowing that God does answer prayers even for other people.

The obvious conclusion is that there are certain things in which we are told to pray for or about because prayer can change the direction or outcome to be different than it would be if prayers were not offered. Thus, it seems prudent to pray in both areas, those that we are confident are conditionals and those about which we are not. We want to pray for the ones that we may be unsure about because we know it may be conditional. Paul could be sure he was praying appropriately. God commands not to do wrong (Eph 5:3–21) and to grow into all things (Eph 4:15). But in areas the Scripture does not explicitly speak, we should pray, making our requests known to God because we know it is the will of God that we do so, and then close with "Your will be done," resting in God's ultimate will for our lives.

Accordingly, we see our prayers are essential for fellowship, God changing us, and because God has so constituted Christianity that some things will be different if we pray than if we do not pray. The prayer for change could relate to a person's spiritual well-being, salvation, spiritual growth, a child's protection, avoiding potential danger like praying for safe travel, marriage protection and growth, finances, health, another person, sharing the gospel, preparing to be used by God, education, a job, a house, and a whole galaxy of other things. We give counsel when someone is facing a challenging issue and say they have to be strong and make the right decision.

But, of course, that only makes sense in a world where some things are not determined. The same understanding is necessary to make sense of all the biblical teachings about prayer. For a determinist to say, well, the Bible says to pray, and so we pray, or we are doing what Paul did does not make compatibilism make biblical sense. If we accept all things are determined, and everything is exactly as God determined it to be at any given moment, the only reason to pray for something to be different or to model after Paul is because that desire was determined as well. But an ordinary reading of the Scripture does not lead to that understanding. We quickly know from Scripture that God does not desire his people to do wrong; therefore, we pray for them to make a right, godly decision, and we can know that is the heart and the mind of God. We do not need to be determined to figure this out.

Can you imagine getting to heaven and finding out that some undesirable events happened that did not have to happen if we had asked? Or to find out a host of things we would have liked to see happen that would have if we had asked? God does not have to spell out every event he has designed as a conditional, which may be a near impossibility in this present world. We do not need that because God's commands about prayer testify to the pervasiveness of conditionals in the world. "Pray without ceasing" (1 Thess 5:17) and for "everything" (Phil 4:6).

It is about understanding God's plan and not missing what he has for us and wants to do through us. When we begin to grasp this dynamic relationship, prayer becomes a part of who we are because we know God has tied doing some things to our choice to ask. We do not know what they all are, but we do know if we do not ask, we will miss out on many things he desires us to experience. Based on the proportionality of events affected by human choice in Scripture, we may even suggest that in a libertarian free world, there are probably far more outcomes tied to our choices, asking and praying and obeying, than not. That being the case, we should pray for all things and rest in "Your will be done."

For God's will to be fully accomplished, we must make our requests known since he commanded that we do so. Our prayers should never be merely for self, but to the best we understand at the moment, they must always be in line with glorifying God. We know we are human and can miss something, which is why we trust in and conclude all prayers with a heart that finds solace in "Your will be done." But we may be equally assured that only praying "Your will be done" does not represent the full biblical teaching of our privilege and responsibility in prayer.

So be encouraged to pray through Scripture, pray devotionally, pray privately and corporately, pray with a few or many, pray for others and ask others to pray for you, but in everything, pray. You don't have to think about what to pray. The number of things that will come to your mind in a day will be between a hundred and a zillion. Don't think about what to pray. Just pray about what you think about. This truth does not replace your prayer list or dedicated times of prayer, but it will help you fulfill the commands to pray about all things all the time.

Ephesians 1:18

Paul prayed for the Ephesians' spiritual growth. He said, "I pray that the eyes of your heart may be enlightened, so that you will know what is the hope of His calling, what are the riches of the glory of His inheritance in the saints" (Eph 1:18). We need to pray for the lost and the saved. We pray for the lost to be saved and the saved to know the fullness of God and his salvation. Additionally, while prayer for an individual is undoubtedly biblical, we see in Jesus' and Paul's prayers for the lost and the saved that they prayed for groups of people. We can and should do both.

Paul said, "And this I pray, that your love may abound still more and more in real knowledge and all discernment" (Phil 1:9). Paul was interceding and praying for others in things that he knew were the will of God for others. We can pray for the spiritual growth of someone. We can pray for a marriage not to end in divorce. We can pray for our child not to be a renegade. Why? Not because the Scripture specifically mentions that marriage or that child, but Scripture teaches us God's heart concerning marriage, God's heart concerning children, and God's heart regarding spiritual growth.

Paul prayed, "We give thanks to God, the Father of our Lord Jesus Christ, praying always for you. . . . For this reason also, since the day we heard of it, we have not ceased to pray for you and to ask that you may be filled with the knowledge of His will in all spiritual wisdom and understanding" (Col 1:3, 9). So again, Paul is interceding for others. We are to pray for others, both lost and saved. Further, our prayers are not in conflict with libertarian free will but rather because of it. Determinism makes prayer incapable of changing outcomes, which is not what we see in Scripture.

While seeing things we have prayed for come to pass surely encourages us and strengthens our faith in prayer, just relying on being able to confirm the results of our prayers for our motivation to pray will limit our prayers. It will limit us to pray, at least passionately, for people and things that will remain within our experiential knowledge. We will have little passion and faithfulness to pray for others and things that are not within our experiential knowledge. Two examples will illustrate this point.

You could hear of a need of someone you do not know. If seeing answered prayer is what motivates you to pray, there will be little motivation to pray about this on the outskirts of your experiential knowledge. Another example could be you see someone or talk with someone with whom you may never have future contact. It could be someone whom you walked by on the street and could see their need, or you felt impressed to pray for their salvation. It could be someone in a restaurant or someone you got to know for a brief time who then moved. We might offer a prayer out of obligation, but the passion and confidence are limited because those kinds of prayers will not provide knowable results. Consequently, seeking motivation solely by being able to witness the results not only limits what we will pray about, but it can also defeat our prayer life for a short duration or even for life.

On the other hand, if we pray because we have learned from events throughout Scripture that sometimes God's blessing is conditioned on our asking, our motivation comes from that understanding. It is not necessary to know how our prayers for others turn out. Therefore, we can passionately pray for people and situations in which we will never know if or how God worked in that particular event. With our motivation drawn from that biblical knowledge, we could be in a box in a dungeon where we never got to see anything happen, and we could pray faithfully, passionately, and energetically for the rest of our lives. But we can be at peace, knowing God does things when we pray that he does not do when we do not. This biblically derived knowledge makes passionate praying not contingent on confirming results but, instead, on how God has constructed the universe.

Prayer is for fellowshipping with God and changing us, but it is also for changing outcomes; even this last aspect deepens our fellowship with God and changes our lives. Knowing there are so many things that can be avoided and so many opportunities that can come because we are praying can energize our prayers. We can be changed to love prayer and fall more in love with the one to whom we make our requests. The experience of prayer changes us, but the change in what we experience from praying in the area of conditionals changes us as well.

Hebrews 13:18–19

Not only are we praying for other people, but we are also asking other people to pray for us. The author of Hebrews said, "Pray for us, for we are sure that we have a good conscience, desiring to conduct ourselves honorably in all things. And I urge you all the more to do this, so that I may be restored to you the sooner." (Heb 13:18–19). Paul wrote half of the New Testament, yet he urgently pleads with others to pray for him (Col 4:3; 1 Thess 5:25). Accordingly, we pray continually, we pray comprehensively, we pray for other people, and we ask them to pray for us. None of these occurrences give the impression that the prayer requests were without the concomitant belief that prayer could affect their situations in a way that would not happen if people did not pray nor that their requests were determined.

James 5:14–16

We are commanded to pray for other people.

> Is anyone among you sick? Then he must call for the elders of the church and they are to pray over him, anointing him with oil in the name of the Lord; and the prayer offered in faith will restore the one who is sick, and the Lord will raise him up, and if he has committed sins, they will be forgiven him. Therefore, confess your sins to one another, and pray for one another so that you may be healed. The effective prayer of a righteous man can accomplish much. (Jas 5:14–16)

There is a place a person gets to when they seriously need intercession. It's not just going to the elders when you get beaten down or are physically or spiritually ill. That last verse is about going to others in the body of Christ and seeking their prayers. We have seen that we should pray about ourselves, but one reason we should ask others to pray for us is sometimes we are weak spiritually, or we are weak physically, and the battle is too much. Sometimes the elders are involved, but this is not limited to just the elders; it gives a place to each of us to pray for each other.

In the past, I have been asked by people to pray for a need, and I would have the best of intentions of doing so later. Contrary to my heart and genuine promise to pray, I often forgot. To avoid this, I began trying to pray for them either at that moment or as soon as we parted company. Many times, I am asked to pray for someone as they are headed somewhere or to do something, so time is of the essence. Since I have practiced praying for them as I walk away, I am far less likely to forget to pray for them and far more likely to remember to pray for them again later. If we say we are going to pray for someone, we should.

15

Can Our Prayers about the Past
Make a Difference?

PRAYING ABOUT THINGS THAT have already happened is more a part of our prayer life than we realize. These prayers can encompass many events, but here a few scenarios. Someone could have asked you to pray for their job interview at one o'clock, but you forgot and did not pray until one-thirty. Your child is traveling, and you pray for their safety, but unbeknownst to you, they were in a building when it caught fire, which preceded your prayer. I am sure you can think of many times you had prayed about something or someone when, in fact, the event or danger you prayed about had passed. Because this is a part of our prayer life, it is important to understand what is possible and impossible. I pray this chapter will encourage you to pray even when something has already happened, whether or not you are aware of the precise details.

You may have prayed for something that has already happened, like the job interview mentioned. Realizing the interview has started or is even over, you may say, I do not know if it will do any good to pray now, but I will go ahead because it cannot hurt anything. This is sort of a hope or a magical approach. You may conclude there is no reason to pray since the event has passed, and it is impossible to change the past. While it is true that we cannot change the past, that does not necessarily mean that our prayers cannot make a difference in the event.

Here is why. Please stick with me because you will learn how prayers may matter, even if we prayed after something has happened. First, neither our prayers nor anything else can change the past. That is called backward causation, and that is impossible.[1] You have probably heard the saying, "it is no use crying over spilled milk." It means the past has happened, and you cannot do anything about it, so move on with your life. Worry about and work on something you can change because you cannot change the past; the milk has already spilled. But our prayers can have an impact on some conditionals that have happened before we pray. These prayers do not change the past after it has happened but rather change what would become the past.

For example, Mike, Betty's husband, goes to the doctor for a cancer screening. Let's say the test will show he does have cancer. So even before the doctor reads the results or delivers the news to the patient, Mike has cancer. Once cancer detection is a part of the past, nothing, not even prayers to God, can change that. Because it is impossible, the milk is already spilled, and you cannot change that fact. You can only clean it up and move on; in other words, treat the cancer.

While it is true that the test is in the past, and as such, it is unchangeable (backward causation), this does not mean that prayer cannot influence some conditionals that take place before we know about them. That our prayers can change outcomes, in this case Mike's diagnosis, is based on the truth that God is essentially omniscient. Consequently, we are not talking about prayers changing the past but instead changing what would have become the past had God not known Betty would pray. Changing what God knew the past would become is possible since God always knows every contingency, the results of libertarian beings making a choice. God eternally knew if Betty would pray for Mike, who went in for cancer testing, albeit after he had already been tested.

The question then becomes, did God design this event to be conditional? That is, did God choose to make whether Mike's test result comes back positive or negative dependent on whether or not Betty prayed for him even though it was after the fact? If so, the positive cancer diagnosis would never occur when it would have had Betty not prayed. Therefore, God is not changing the past, or holding a false belief in eternity about the future (what would become the past in time), but the prayer did change the outcome. Prayer did not change the past, but it changed what would

1. As noted earlier, God could intervene and override the natural order of time (Josh 10:1–14; Judg 7:17, 36–40; Isa 38:8), but in the normal course of time, barring such a supernatural intervention, backward causation cannot happen. Without a miraculous intervention of God, backward causation is impossible.

become known as the past. God always knew Mike would be diagnosed with cancer if Betty did not pray (in this scenario), but he knew Betty would pray, belatedly so, and he would answer her prayers, so the outcome would be that Mike did not have cancer. Since God always knew about Betty's prayer, he answered that prayer so that Mike never had cancer. Therefore, the prayer changed what became the past but not the past. Consequently, if Betty would not have prayed, the diagnosis would have said Mike has cancer, but since God knew she would pray, albeit after the test had been done, God answered the prayer before the test (based on his foreknowledge Betty would pray) and the test came back negative.

In like manner, regarding not only prayer but also equally true of all acts of a libertarian free being, if I had chosen (at the last second) to do A instead of B, God would not have held the belief that I would do B. He would have eternally known I would do A. I do not change the past by making a different decision, but the past is different because I chose differently, and God comprehended free choice in his creative plan. One's ability to pray and effect changes is not equivalent to changing the past once it has happened, only to change what would have been the past had I chosen differently or prayed for a different outcome. Therefore, it is possible for prayer and choices to change what would have become the past had I not prayed because God chose to comprehend that prayer or choice in his conditional plans.

This understanding helps us know how our prayers may work in a situation that has already occurred without resorting to committing to the fallacy of believing we can change the past after it has already happened. It can help us understand how God can eternally know what the future will be, yet our prayers can change future outcomes. First, it would have to be conditional outcomes that God determined to be affected by people's influence. Second, our prayers' change of results in a conditional does not mean God changed the future, but rather God changed what the future would have been without the prayer to what it will be with our prayer. He always knew whether the prayer would be offered or not offered about that future event, whether he had created it as a conditional, and, therefore, he always knew the event would happen differently if we prayed than if we did not pray.

For example, you are going to interview for a job you want. So, as a Christian, you quite understandably pray you will get the job. Consider the two possible outcomes. One, you don't get the job. The reason could be because getting the job was not conditional but a determined event, in which case, prayers and human involvement do not affect the outcome. As you recall, other than the conditionals the Bible addresses explicitly, we don't know them for sure. Or if getting the job was conditional, it could be you prayed for God's perfect will even if it meant not getting the job. In this case, when all the facts are known, it was better for you not to get the job, even though it does not seem that way at the moment. You chose to trust God rather than assume you were sure this was his will, which is always the best.

Two, you get the job. This could mean that getting the job was conditional. The one component that changed the outcome from you not getting the job to you getting the job is that you prayed about it. This outcome does not mean you changed the future, but rather your prayer, as eternally comprehended by God, changed what the future would have been if you had not prayed to what it is because you prayed, and God always knew that.

Let me clarify with one more example of going to the store. God always knew that you would go to the store today. Such knowledge by God does not mean you cannot refrain from going to the store. It is that if you go to the store, God would have always known that, and if you change your mind at the last micro-second and do not go to the store, God would have always known that. It is helpful for God's glory to understand how prayer and choices affect the past and future in light of God's omniscience. Remember, when we talk about God's nature, he is a little bit complicated, at least to understand from a human vantage point. He is, after all, the only being who knows specifically what almost eight billion minds are thinking at any given second, and he has eternally known that.

Tyre and Sidon provide a biblical account of how choices in the past would have made the future different, and God would have known that. Jesus had done a lot of miracles and is excoriating the unrepentant cities for not believing.

> Then He began to denounce the cities in which most of His miracles were done because they did not repent. "Woe to you, Chorazin! Woe to you, Bethsaida! For if the miracles had occurred in Tyre and Sidon which occurred in you, they would have repented long ago in sackcloth and ashes. Nevertheless I say to you, it will be more tolerable for Tyre and Sidon in the day of judgment than for you. And you, Capernaum, will not be exalted to heaven, will you? You will descend to Hades; for if the miracles had occurred in Sodom which occurred in you, it would have remained to this day.

Nevertheless I say to you that it will be more tolerable for the land of Sodom in the day of judgment, than for you." (Matt 11:20–24)

Notice the conditionals introduced by if; if Tyre, Sidon, and Sodom had seen what Chorazin, Bethsaida, and Capernaum saw, they would have repented and remained. They did not see them, and therefore, they did not remain. The facts of history (they repent and remain) would have been different, and God would have always known they would.

16

Biblical and Applicable Examples of God Overriding Man's Free Will

God's Sovereignty and Man's Free Will

THIS CHAPTER CONSIDERS LIBERTARIAN free will, choice, and prayer in light of God's sovereignty. God can and does, at times, overrule our free will. But that does not mean our free will is eliminated. This topic creates much confusion. People think if you cannot do everything you want, then you do not have free will. They believe if God overrides your free will, you lose your free will. No, it only means you are not responsible for that choice, and your range of options may have changed. For example, the government could imprison a Christian because he is a Christian, and, of course, this would not be the option the Christian would have chosen for himself. Even though he is in prison and is not free to do all he could before being forcibly imprisoned, he still has his free will; he just does not have the range of options he had before being taken to prison.

A simple but accurate understanding of libertarian and compatible freedom is, even with the same past, a libertarian free being can decide to act or refrain in the moral moment of decision, and whichever option he chooses, he could have chosen differently.[1] In contrast, according to compatibilism, given the same past, a compatibly free being cannot choose differently than he did choose in the moral moment of decision. He freely

---

1. This ability does not have to be true in every circumstance, only some.

chooses according to his greatest desire, but his greatest desire is determined; hence, he makes a determined free choice.

If God overrules a person's free will, it does not eliminate his libertarian freedom. It merely reminds us God is sovereign. As I have said before, libertarian free will is a force created by God, but like all other forces, it is under the sovereign rule of God, and he can, therefore, override it at any time and as often as he so desires. When this happens, a person's decision is not because of God's persuasiveness but because God caused the person to make a particular decision. You may be responsible for the decisions that brought you to that point, and you are responsible for decisions after that, but you are not responsible for that particular decision that God caused.

Let me give this example to illustrate. Let's say Bob chooses to rob a store. He is caught, taken to court, found guilty, and taken to prison. He is not incarcerated because he decided to go to prison, but he did choose to commit the robbery that resulted in others taking him to prison. He is incarcerated because the local authorities overrode Bob's free will, but he is responsible for the robbery and breaking the law. He is not responsible for the choice to be in prison because he would have chosen to commit the theft and not go to prison. The legal system is responsible for Bob being incarcerated. So, the police get credit for him being imprisoned, not him. We may applaud Bob being in prison, but we do not applaud Bob for putting himself in prison.

Another example might be if you have a small child who throws a temper tantrum and she is sent to her room because of it, you are overriding her free will. She exercised her free will to throw a tantrum, even in light of possible punishment. She wanted the tantrum to result in her getting her way, but you vetoed her desire by making her go to her room against her will. Now, she can submit to her loss of freedom by walking to her room, or she can resist and be carried kicking and screaming. But either way, she will go. However, she does not lose her free will. She only lost the freedom about the decision of whether or not to be sent to her room. She now must choose whether her punishment will teach her a lesson or if she will continue to do wrong.

Thus, it is easy to see that God, as sovereign, can override libertarian free will. Even humans can override other humans' free will, at times, without a person losing their libertarian freedom. The beliefs that free will is lost if it is overridden and libertarian freedom allows a person to do anything are based on a misunderstanding of libertarianism.

Biblical Examples of God Overriding Man's Free Will

Genesis 20:1–6

This passage concerns Abraham and Sarah and their lying about their relationship. Both Abraham and Sarah said they were brother and sister. He lied about her because he was seeking to protect himself. He had acted this way once before, but he had not learned his lesson (Gen 12:11–13). The passage says,

> Now Abraham journeyed from there toward the land of the Negev, and settled between Kadesh and Shur; then he sojourned in Gerar. Abraham said of Sarah, his wife, "She is my sister." So Abimelech, king of Gerar, sent and took Sarah. But God came to Abimelech in a dream of the night and said to him, "Behold, you are a dead man because of the woman whom you have taken, for she is married." Now Abimelech had not come near her; and he said, "Lord, will You slay a nation, even though blameless? Did he not himself say to me, 'She is my sister?' And she herself said, 'He is my brother.' In the integrity of my heart and the innocence of my hands I have done this." Then God said to him in the dream, "Yes, I know that in the integrity of your heart you have done this, and I also kept you from sinning against Me; therefore I did not let you touch her." (Gen 20:1–6)

The story is pretty straightforward. God speaks to Abimelech in a couple of dreams and says, "You are a dead man." That is about as clear as a message can get. But Abimelech's defense before God is that both Abraham and Sarah lied to him, claiming to be brother and sister and not husband and wife. Because they lied, Abimelech declares that he is innocent of knowingly taking a married woman, and he is correct.

Further, he "had not come near her," sexually speaking. God even recognizes the integrity of Abimelech's heart, meaning everything Abimelech said was true. These words do not mean Abimelech was innocent in his heart, but only that he was correct that he had not knowingly taken a married woman into his harem or come near her. But he did take her into his harem, which indicates sinful intentions.[2] Then God says, "I also kept you from sinning against Me; therefore, I did not let you touch her."

2. Friedrich Keil says, "But that God should have admitted that he had acted 'in innocence of heart,' and yet should have proceeded at once to tell him that he could only remain alive through the intercession of Abraham, that is to say, through his obtaining forgiveness of a sin that was deserving of death, is a proof that God treated him as capable

It is possible, based on the nature of God, man, and free will, that God kept Abimelech from touching Sarah by working persuasively and circumstantially. Working in this way would not be overriding Abimelech's free will but merely applying pressure that left the choice to Abimelech. However, it seems God would have done more if necessary. It is also possible that though Abimelech did not approach Sarah, God had determined that he would not permit any kind of relationship between Abimelech and Sarah even if Abimelech tried to start one, or that God had already prevented Abimelech by overriding his will. In this case, that God kept him from sinning would entail God forcibly stopping him. The latter of the two possibilities would mean that God either overrode Abimelech's will or that he would have if Abimelech chose to approach Sarah. It appears to me that God's words, "I also kept you from sinning," indicate God had already overridden his free will.[3]

This situation is a demonstration of God protecting all three of them from behind the scenes, so to speak. It seems God intended to protect Abraham and Sarah, but by doing so, he also protected Abimelech by giving him a way not to die for what he had done.[4] By application, we should not miss that God may similarly protect us in ways that are not apparent to us at the time. He was protecting Abimelech, who had not touched Sarah, and therefore, had not sinned. God also was protecting Abraham and Sarah, who had sinned by lying, which, unfortunately, might be true of us at times. We get ourselves into a predicament, and God, by his grace, still rescues us. God was protecting Sarah when Abraham was not. Accordingly, we may feel alone or may have contributed to the situation we are in, but as believers, we are never alone.

God then said to Abimelech, "Now therefore, restore the man's wife, for he is a prophet, and he will pray for you and you will live. But if you do not restore her, know that you shall surely die, you and all who are yours" (Gen 20:7). This passage is the first time the word "prophet" is used in the Old Testament, and it is used of Abraham. For our study, here is the

---

of deeper moral discernment and piety." Keil and Delitzsch, *Pentateuch*, 153.

3. Some believe God hindered Abimelech through making him sick. For example, Friedrich Keil says, "Abimelech, who had not yet come near her, because God had hindered him by illness (vv. 6 and 17)." Keil and Delitzsch, *Pentateuch*, 153.

4. If relations between Abimelech and Sarah took place, that would cast doubt on whether Abraham would be the biological father of their forthcoming child Isaac. God overrides the free will of man to accomplish his salvation plan for the world when necessary.

question. Was Abimelech going to live because he had a clear conscience? No. Because he was guiltless? No. Because he did not sin with Sarah? No. God is clear; he would let Abimelech live because Abraham would pray for him if he restored Sarah to him. His living was conditioned on Abraham praying for him. Abraham's praying for him was conditioned on Abimelech choosing to restore Sarah.

This passage illustrates God's involvement in a dynamic human interaction with both determinism and free choice. The deterministic aspect of the situation seems as if their free will choices might thwart God's salvation plan. Remember, God's permissive will allows us free choice, but God will not let us destroy his overall redemptive plan. The narrative involves three people, the sin of lying, and probably Abimelech's sin of thinking it is OK for a king to take unmarried women into his harem. Abimelech alone acted with integrity, as far as the physical actions that are referred to, but we do not know his thoughts because the text only tells us about his actions. But God knows everything, and he chose to intervene. Similarly, at times, it may seem like a person's conscience keeps her from sinning since God does not usually inform us about his interventions, but it could be God overriding the person's moral freedom. That can be God providing a way out of temptation as he did with Abimelech (1 Cor 10:13). It just may be a choice we can and should make, but as seen here, it also can include God protecting us from ourselves.

It is important to note God makes Abimelech's life hinge on Abraham's prayer (v. 7). But Abraham's prayer hinged on whether or not Abimelech chose to restore Sarah. The passage gives every indication that he could decide to restore her, be prayed for, and live, or he could decide not to restore her, not be prayed for, and die. Note the conditional nature of the promise, "But if you do not restore her, know that you shall surely die" (v. 7).

Accordingly, this passage is a mixture of the free will of Abraham and Sarah choosing to sin by lying (God has no part in leading, enticing, or causing someone to sin, Jas 1:13), determinism (God forcibly restrained Abimelech from sinning, v. 6), Abimelech then exercising free will in choosing whether or not to restore Sarah (v. 7), and Abimelech's deliverance being dependent on Abraham's prayer (v. 7).[5] I believe the passage gives a great

5. You find a similarly complex event in Acts 2:23 about the crucifixion of our Lord Jesus Christ. It is a mixture of a predetermined plan of God for Christ to die for man's sin with uncertain events—people making free will choices. As seen in this passage with Abimelech, events do not have to be made up of exclusively determined or free otherwise choices. They can be a mixture of the two.

insight into the complexities of human relationships and prayer that might be found in other situations. However, the circumstances and reasoning will vary according to the situation.

I see no reason why a similar type of complexity cannot exist in many human life events. I mean scenarios where some choices may be made by the free will of one or all of the persons involved while other outcomes are made by God overruling one or more persons' free will. Another encouraging application is it reminds us that God's choicest saints still sinned, and yet God used them mightily in his salvation plan. Thus, while we take sin seriously, we must not fall into despair when the grace of God is available.

We can see the conditional nature of the resolution of this event. The resolution was conditioned on Abraham praying for Abimelech, which was conditioned on Abimelech returning Sarah untouched. It was not enough for Abimelech to return Sarah, but Abraham had to pray for him. A further application drawn from this passage is that since we know God has conditioned the outcome of some situations on our choices and prayers, we can understand that God has conditioned some events we are in with others being resolved or turning out differently if we pray for one or more of the people involved.

As humans, we are involved in many relationships and interactions that include varying degrees of complexity, which should always have us praying for wisdom (Jas 1:5). We should also pray for those with whom we are involved. This encounter reminds us that some situations may even be more complicated than we think. The situation may involve the free choice to sin, the consequence of that sin, the integrity of the person involved, God preventing or causing certain things to avoid worse outcomes, the free choices of others involved that help the situation, and our prayers playing a role in the result. We know of this situation with Abraham and Sarah because God revealed it to us in Scripture, but we do not have a revelation on everything. The description in this passage may suggest it happens elsewhere; I think we are safe to assume similar situations do arise. You may get to heaven and find out this person is alive because you prayed when God impressed you to pray. That is why, in part, we are trusting that God impresses us, leading us with his Spirit and his word, and we are praying continuously, comprehensively, and spiritually.

Daniel 3:19–20

This is the story about King Nebuchadnezzar and the three Hebrews. It is another case where there is the exercise of free will and God overriding free will. We speak of God's permissive will, by which we mean God allows people to choose to do things that are not his desired will for them and, therefore, is not what is best for them in the long run. But, he will not allow that freedom to thwart his salvation plan even if he must override their free will

I want to highlight a few verses that relate to the topic of this book. Daniel says, "Then Nebuchadnezzar was filled with wrath, and his facial expression was altered toward Shadrach, Meshach and Abed-nego. He answered by giving orders to heat the furnace seven times more than it was usually heated. He commanded certain valiant warriors who were in his army to tie up Shadrach, Meshach and Abed-nego in order to cast them into the furnace of blazing fire" (Dan 3:19–20).

Nebuchadnezzar had an image built and commanded all of Babylon to bow and worship at signaled times (vv. 1–5). Refusing to do so brought the penalty of death by being cast into the furnace (vv. 5–6). Nebuchadnezzar was apprised that Shadrach, Meshach, and Abed-nego were not bowing down, which enraged the king (vv. 12–13), and he sent for them. Then the king reiterated the command and gave them another chance to bow down and worship or face being burned alive in the furnace (vv. 15–18). They responded with those familiar words, "If it be so, our God whom we serve is able to deliver us from the furnace of blazing fire. . . . But even if He does not, let it be known to you, O king, that we are not going to serve your gods or worship the golden image that you have set up" (Dan 3:17, 18).

The sin of the king and the faith of the three Hebrews give no indication of being determined. All evidence is that all made libertarian free choices. That is why we think Nebuchadnezzar is sinful, and that is the reason God judged him. The steadfast faith of the three Hebrews in the face of a horrific death has been recited for millennia to encourage others to be faithful in trials. None of which makes sense or conveys such meaning if Calvinism's micro-determinism is true. For then, they all just acted as they were predetermined to do. They made no bold and faithful choices in which compromise was an option any more than Nebuchadnezzar chose to sin when he could have chosen to act justly. Everything is happening according to God's determined script.

Nebuchadnezzar chose to have the furnace heated seven times hotter than usual. He commanded that Shadrach, Meshach, and Abed-nego be tied up to be cast into the fire. Nebuchadnezzar is making several freewill choices that are bringing about one outcome that would have and could have been different if he had chosen differently. The outcomes of building the image, commanding image worship, heating the fire so hot that it would kill a person instantaneously, and Shadrach, Meshach, and Abed-nego being thrown into the furnace are all the result of free will choices. There is no indication in the passage that these were determined actions and outcomes.

Yet, what Nebuchadnezzar thought he could control was whether or not the three Hebrews burned. To his shock, they did not burn. "Then Nebuchadnezzar the king was astounded and stood up in haste; he said to his high officials, 'Was it not three men we cast bound into the midst of the fire?' They replied to the king, 'Certainly, O king.' He said, 'Look! I see four men loosed and walking about in the midst of the fire without harm, and the appearance of the fourth is like a son of the gods!'" (Dan 3:24–25). Now, the three Hebrews' famous words of faith and this Christophany is what garners most of our attention in this passage, and rightfully so. But in keeping with our study, I want to focus on the choices that were made.

Nebuchadnezzar chose to kill the Hebrews. He did so as the most powerful man in the world at the time. But God said no. God did not override Nebuchadnezzar's freedom to make the fire seven times hotter, nor to stop him from casting the Hebrews into the fire, but he overrode his free choice to burn them to death.

"Then Nebuchadnezzar came near to the door of the furnace of blazing fire; he responded and said, 'Shadrach, Meshach and Abed-nego, come out, you servants of the Most High God, and come here!' Then Shadrach, Meshach and Abed-nego came out of the midst of the fire" (Dan 3:26). What changed his wrath to destroy them to a request to come out of the fire? It was God's determinative act to protect the Hebrews from Nebuchadnezzar's free choice of wrath. Kings have the idea that they are sovereign. The title of a king is sovereign, for his position is to protect his people. As the true sovereign of the universe, God is concerned about protecting his people and carrying out his salvation plan in time and space. In an unusual demonstration of God's power over Nebuchadnezzar's power, Nebuchadnezzar vividly and shockingly sees that truth.

Daniel 4:28–33

This section of Daniel provides another interplay of God overriding human freedom, determinism, and man exercising his libertarian free will. Dan 4:4–27 records that Nebuchadnezzar had a dream that troubled him. He called for the wise men to tell him the dream's meaning, and Daniel interpreted the dream. The vision was about Nebuchadnezzar's pride and God's plan to humble him. Daniel called on Nebuchadnezzar to repent, but he did not. That leads us to this passage that tells us that Nebuchadnezzar did not repent, and the vision did come true.

> All this happened to Nebuchadnezzar, the king. Twelve months later, he was walking on the roof of the royal palace of Babylon. The king reflected and said, "Is this not Babylon the great, which I myself have built as a royal residence by the might of my power and for the glory of my majesty?" While the word was in the king's mouth, a voice came from heaven, saying, "King Nebuchadnezzar, to you it is declared: sovereignty has been removed from you, and you will be driven away from mankind, and your dwelling place will be with the beasts of the field. You will be given grass to eat like cattle, and seven periods of time will pass over you until you recognize that the Most High is ruler over the realm of mankind and bestows it on whomever He wishes." The word concerning Nebuchadnezzar was immediately fulfilled, and he was driven away from mankind and began eating grass like cattle, and his body was drenched with the dew of heaven until his hair had grown like eagles' feathers and his nails like birds' claws. (Dan 4:28–33)

Notice Nebuchadnezzar, at this point, can do nothing to stop God overruling his free will. His freewill choice was to continue to reign and revel in his glory, but God said Nebuchadnezzar's sovereignty "has been removed," and "you will be driven away from mankind." He went on to tell him that he would live like an animal. By every indication, Nebuchadnezzar had the opportunity to choose to be a humble king. Then even in his arrogance, he was given a chance to choose to repent (4:27), but he did not. Then he lost the ability to choose to humble himself so that God's judgment would not come on him. And God says Nebuchadnezzar would stay like a beast until he recognized God as sovereign. The vision revealed that God would restore him one day, but only after he realized that God is the true sovereign. God is sovereign by nature; all others are such because God deems them to be over a particular sphere for a specific time.

The passage goes on to say,

> But at the end of that period, I, Nebuchadnezzar, raised my eyes
> toward heaven and my reason returned to me, and I blessed the
> Most High and praised and honored Him who lives forever; For
> His dominion is an everlasting dominion, And His kingdom en-
> dures from generation to generation. All the inhabitants of the
> earth are accounted as nothing, But He does according to His will
> in the host of heaven And among the inhabitants of earth; And no
> one can ward off His hand Or say to Him, 'What have You done?'"
> (Dan 4:34–35)

That last part is critical to understand that Nebuchadnezzar indeed
recognized that God has no superiors, but he does. When Nebuchadnezzar's reason returns, he rightly recognizes God for who he is. He realizes
what God can do, and he, as king of Babylon, was no match for him. By
being driven away from everything and forcibly humbled, Nebuchadnezzar
recognized the truth that nothing challenges the sovereignty of God.

"Now I, Nebuchadnezzar, praise, exalt and honor the King of heaven,
for all His works are true and His ways just, and He is able to humble those
who walk in pride" (Dan 4:37). That is a personal testimony. God's plan
was not for Nebuchadnezzar's harm but for his good. Think about it. Was
Nebuchadnezzar better off thinking he was sovereign, and he could do anything he wants? Or was he better off to be humbled before God? The latter
is the better of the two outcomes. At first glance, it was judgment alone.
But to think it was just judgment is to miss the merciful work of God in
his judgment. What God did to Nebuchadnezzar made him better off and
improved the lives of the people over whom he ruled. Everyone who reads
or hears of this encounter between Nebuchadnezzar and God also would
have an opportunity to be more fortunate.

Such is the same with the judgment God brought on Pharaoh. God
humbled Pharaoh so that Israel, Pharaoh, and the Egyptians would know
God was God and not Pharaoh (Exod 6:6–7; 7:5; 9:14; 10:1–2; 13:14–16;
14:4, 18), and he used Pharaoh to make his name declared throughout the
whole earth (Exod 9:16).

Like Abimelech's event, this one is also a mixture of free will choices
and God overriding the king's free will. Nebuchadnezzar made many free
will choices to revel and walk in sinful pride. He also made a free will decision to repent. But it was the sovereign overriding of the king's will in which
God drove him from living like a king in the palace to living like an animal

in the wilderness that God used to bring him to the realization that God is sovereign. I think we can all easily see that it would make no sense if God predetermined him to walk in pride and sin and then punish him to break his pride. That turns this event into a theater of puppetry.

Applicable Examples of God Overriding Man's Free Will

In exceptional circumstances, I can see the validity of praying for God to intervene, even overruling a person's will. An example might be a situation in which a person seeks to harm himself or others. Because of the nature of libertarian free will, when God or anyone overrides a person's free will, the person is not responsible for that choice. It appears in Scripture this is not the normal way God interacts with humans or permits them to relate to each other; therefore, applying this to everyday life, I would assume the same. In other words, God created man with libertarian choice so man could make choices between accessible options and be responsible for his choices. Choices are involved in the ordinary course of life, but God can and does override these choices when they may subvert his creation-redemption plan, as we have seen in various biblical examples in this chapter and throughout the book.

Picture a situation where a child is abducted. What do we pray? God, protect the child. And I will tell you; I am not worried about the abductor's free will. And if the prayer to protect the child overrides the abductor's freedom, that is fine! I believe God may very well override the abductors' free will. God may lead him to make a mistake, or he may inexplicably, at least as far as we know, let the child go. We will never know the truth of everything that actually happened in some situations until we get to heaven. It could also be that God worked persuasively through someone or conditions changing, so the man decided to let the child go. It could be that God overrode the man's free will, and therefore, he made the right choice. Although people may mistakenly give him credit for doing the right thing, he does not get credit because he did not make the choice of his own volition. But the result is the child was protected. I think there are times like this, maybe even more than we can think.

Just listen to our prayers as parents. Sometimes we are totally uninterested in whether our children have a choice. If our six-year-old child tried to run in front of a car, thought she could drive a car, wanted to walk around the mall on her own, or any of countless other dangerous choices, we would stop her with necessary force without one whit of concern about her free will in the matter. We do it because we love her.

The potential of praying for God to override another's freedom when there is a threat or danger does not mean that we can control other people, for that is more than what God chose to do when he created humanity with libertarian freedom, even though he is capable. Praying is not magic. Praying that incorporates God overriding another person's free will is not praying because we want them to merely act differently or out of a heart to control them. That would not be a valid reason, and I do not think it is the kind of prayer that glorifies God.

God is capable of creating determined beings, and some believe he did. But I think the Bible is clear that he did not choose to create determined humans. God's permissive will allows people to freely choose what is not his best for them and what at times is not good for others. That is the nature of having libertarian moral freedom. Adam and Eve are the exemplars of this. And we have chosen many times similarly. Being created with the ability to choose between options is both a privilege and a responsibility, as is all freedom.

If God overrides an individual's freedom at a particular time, that does not mean he loses his free will. For example, your three-year-old child does not want to go to her room. What do you do? You pick her up and carry her to her room. At that moment, she does not get a free choice for that decision, but she does not lose her free will. She just lost the freedom to choose differently on that occasion. The child would not be accountable for the decision to go to her room. The mother made that decision, and she is responsible for that decision. The mother could have chosen to spank, assign extra chores, or not to punish, among many other options before her. The child was only responsible for acting in such a way that would result in her mother overriding her free will.

If God answered prayers that overrode someone's libertarian freedom in a particular decision, it would mean the person is not morally responsible for that specific decision. It would also mean the outcome would be different because we prayed. Another consideration in praying for others or events is that while at times our prayer changes the result, it may also sometimes be an example of praying for God to do precisely what he is already going to do even if we did not pray. At that moment, we have simply prayed what God was going to do without our prayers. However, just as we do not know all things that are determined or made conditional by God, we do not know all of these times either. Because of that uncertainty, we are all the more committed to praying.

Praying for God to override someone's free will could be anything from the overthrow of a brutal regime, using force to protect us from someone who means us evil, or causing someone who is seeking to hurt a loved one to have a change of mind. You could intercede by praying that God would protect you, your family, or whomever from lurking evil. While such a change of mind not being freely made would mean the person is not responsible for the morally good change of mind, it does mean that God did work and change the outcome because you prayed if it was a conditional outcome. An example is a phrase in the Lord's Prayer that says lead us not into temptation, but deliver us from evil. "Deliver" is the Greek word *ruomai*, which is a strong word. It is "to rescue from danger, with the implication that the danger in question is severe and acute."[6] That could range from protecting to delivering one right out of the clutches of death.

Another example might be a mom praying for her children to avoid making harmful, irrevocable decisions, which they might have chosen had she not prayed. Everyone makes bad decisions, and sometimes God will use those for good. But some bad decisions lead to permanent consequences, and as parents, I believe we can and should pray that God would protect our children from making irrevocable bad decisions. I know we did, and I do not regret it one bit. I think it is the prayer of a concerned parent who seeks God's protection of those he has given us from making decisions from which there is no return.[7] God's protection may involve him working persuasively, protectively, or even overrulingly, and we leave that with him.

As an example, your teenager may be planning to go out with friends, but at the last minute decides not to go. The friends get in a car wreck, and everyone is killed. Your teen is later sharing his testimony and telling how he didn't get in the car. That choice might have been because of his free will, but it might have been that God overrode his choice or that someone was praying for God to protect him from himself. And now he has lived to hear the gospel, to have different influences in his life, and, as a result, he gets saved. And this becomes a part of his testimony. We will not always know for sure whether God worked overrulingly, persuasively,

6. Louw and Nida, *Greek-English Lexicon*, 240.

7. Choosing to commit suicide by jumping off a cliff is an example of an irrevocable decision.

or circumstantially. Still, we know that it could have been a conditional in which our prayer made the difference (Heb 10:38).

The same thing would apply when your child is dating someone, but you do not believe that person is a good match. Don't give up. Love is a tough bond to break through. Pray for God to either change the person your child is in love with to be someone that would honor God with his life, or pray that God would incline your child's heart away from that person. Let's say that God overrides your daughter's free will, and she lives long enough to meet someone who is a great match; she would be grateful for your prayers and God's intervention.

This illustration reminds us that if God overrides someone's free will, it does not mean the person does not benefit. He would often benefit from having opportunities to make good choices that he would not have if his freedom had not been overridden. He could be spared negative or even horrific consequences that would have happened had his will not been overridden, and he is, thereby, able to make future morally right and spiritually responsible decisions. The boy who chose not to get in the car or the girl who was dating someone that would later be a dangerous husband would not care if God overrode their free will. They're just glad they didn't get in a situation that destroyed their lives, and they now have an opportunity to make better choices.

We are contemplating prayer, choice, and the mind and heart of God. We see similar situations, but we cannot prove exactly what transpired in sparing the ones for whom we prayed. We hear of astonishing stories—people delivered in extraordinary ways. Who knows how many of those could be the outcome of someone praying and God working circumstantially, persuasively, or even overrulingly. Because someone interceded in prayer, the outcome is different than it seemed like it was going to be.

I believe we will get to heaven and find out things that happened because we prayed and things that could have happened if we had prayed. Consequently, we need to pray continually about all things (1 Thess 5:17; Phil 4:6). We know based on the conditionals and promises of Scripture, God does often make a difference in outcomes because we pray. It is inestimable how much protection, relational or marital healing, financial blessing, ministry enhancement, witnessing wisdom, and physical and spiritual healing God does and desires to do in response to prayer if we will ask (Jas 4:2).

As I recall, I was either twelve or thirteen years old when I was offered a ride home from the roller-skating rink late one night by two older guys on a motorcycle (they were going to crowd me on). For whatever reason, I did not get on, and I decided to wait for my dad. I watched them drive down the highway, and then, about a half-mile away, I saw a massive explosion in the direction they had gone.

At the time, I did not know it was them. All I could see was an enormous explosion and fire. Since my dad did not end up coming to pick me up, I started my several-mile walk home. As I approached the place where the explosion happened, I realized it was the guys on the motorcycle, and it killed both of them. The explosion was because they hit a car driven by a drunk who turned in front of them into a beer tavern. Now I don't know if I made a choice, someone prayed for me, or God overrode my free will. Frankly, I have never worried about that. I am just happy I did not die at that time and miss what God has given me since. Other than those described in Scripture, we can never be sure if a situation is conditional. But we can know for sure God answers prayer, even, at times, by working overrulingly of someone's free will so that things turn out differently because we prayed.

What we have seen through all of these situations is that most often, God gives us a choice to obey or not to obey. There is a choice to pray or not to pray. There is a choice to commit evil or not to commit evil. And with each option, there are proportional consequences. We also have seen that God can and does, at times, override a person's libertarian freedom to fulfill his plan or answer prayer. It seems these generally have to do with the propagation of his kingdom on earth or the protection of someone from someone else or themselves. We have also seen that we find people exercising the power of otherwise choice, and God overriding other choices or determining some aspects within the same event in Scripture.

There are only two choices when it comes to Scripture, even though Calvinists frequently speaking libertarianly create inconsistencies in true Calvinism, which clouds this truth. There are two approaches to man's responsibility.[8] One is that man has compatible moral freedom (compatibilism), which means that determinism and moral responsibility are compatible. Everything is determined, but a person is morally responsible because he is considered to have made a free moral decision if he chooses

---

8. There is a third known as determinism, sometimes called "strong" determinism, but neither Extensivists nor Calvinists believe in that.

according to his greatest desire. But in compatibilism, without exception, his greatest desire is determined.

Consequently, it is true and most accurate to say that Calvinism makes a person's choice a determined free choice in compatibilism. His choice will always be what it has been eternally determined to be. Therefore, his choice does not change the course of his next predetermined choosing or outcome. It does not originate a new sequence of events. In the moral moment of choosing, a person could not have chosen differently than he did given that he has the same past because the past determines the desire from which he freely chose. If a person rapes, it was determined that he do so. If a person stops a rape, he was determined to do so. If a person chooses holiness, it was determined by God. If a person chooses immorality, it was determined by God. If a person decides to pray, it was determined by God. If a person decides not to pray, it was determined by God. It is all by God's unchangeable design. I know that it is difficult to accept, but that is the truth if a person wants to speak consistently with Calvinism and its moral perspective of compatibilism. God's permissive will is as determined as everything else, and therefore, the thought that there is the opportunity for otherwise choice is an illusion. It does not exist even one time in a compatible moral belief system.

The second approach is that man has libertarian moral freedom (libertarianism), which means that determinism and moral responsibility are not compatible. A person is considered to make a free choice so long as he could have chosen differently in the moral moment of decision, even with the same past. He can choose to act or refrain. His past can influence his choice, but it is not determinative or causal. The person actually deliberates, decides between various available options, and his decision can change the course of his future. It does initiate a new sequence of events.

The future would be different if he chose to do otherwise, a choice that was in his power at the moment of decision. If a person sins, he did not have to and should have chosen not to. But because he sinned, he will be judged. This is the Extensivist's perspective, which permits man's otherwise choice, God's determining of certain things, and God overriding man's libertarian freedom as he desires. God's permissive will allows us to make choices that may not be his desire or best for us.

In this book, I have sought to make two things crystal clear; first, that God has constituted his world to include some things that he has determined, which cannot be influenced by human choices or prayers, while other things are conditioned based on if we ask in prayer or not; human choices and our prayers can affect these conditionals. If we pray, God will work so that the outcome of the conditional we prayed about will be different than if we did not pray, whereas if we do not pray, he will not change the outcome (Jas 4:2b), and we will miss out on what he desired to do if only we would have asked. Since we do not know everything that is determined or everything conditional, we should be eager to pray about *everything, all the time,* just as he commanded (Phil 4:6; 1 Thess 5:17). We ask because we know it is God's will that we do, and we should entrust everything to him and his goodness by resting in our prayer, "Your will be done."

Second, Calvinism's compatible moral freedom wherein everything is micro-determined leaves us with a Bible that makes little meaningful sense when read normally and a God who seems incapable of communicating that everything is really predetermined. Or even worse, a God who intentionally deceives his people into thinking their choices, prayers, and behaviors matter in such a way that outcomes could have been different if we would, by his grace, have chosen differently.

Therefore, we should make our requests known to God because it is his will that we do and because we know that some things will turn out differently if we pray than if we do not pray (John 16:23–24)!

APPENDIX 1

Calvinism Makes Conditional Statements and Commands Nonsensical

An Expected Reply

THE CALVINIST MAY RESPOND that I err when I say determinism (compatible style) makes conditionals nonsensical. They would probably base this on the idea that, according to compatibilism, man is considered to make a free choice to meet or not meet the condition as long as he chooses according to his greatest desire. Therefore, conditionals are a part of God's determined process. That is to say, choosing to meet or not meet the condition was still a free choice even though they could not have chosen otherwise in the moral moment of decision. According to compatibilism, the person who was determined to meet the condition did so by a free choice. Concerning the person who was predetermined not to meet the condition, he still made a free choice. However, each free choice was based on a predetermined greatest desire; therefore, each person made a predetermined free choice, which could not have been different from what it was in the moral moment of decision; thus, there was not anything really conditional in the encounter between the determined person and the conditional in Scripture.

Further, they may contend that it is logically possible to hold people morally responsible for what they cannot do. For example, a gambler may acquire a massive debt that is so large he cannot pay it off, but his debtors still require him to pay it off. In like manner, God's requirement of the condition to be met by those who cannot satisfy it is not illogical—nonsensical.

My response is that yes, it is logically possible for someone to be unable to meet an obligation and yet responsible. But we are not talking merely about what man can do on his own without God; in Scripture, God is not inactive, thereby leaving man on his own. To take the gambler illustration further, a benefactor could come along and assume the gamblers' debt and pay it off for him. Although unable to pay the debt himself, he can benefit from this gift.[1] This type of gift is more reflective of what we see in Scripture that God did for humanity. He grace enabled the people for whom Christ died (John 1:29; Heb 2:9; Titus 2:11; 1 John 2:2) to receive salvation by trusting him (Eph 2:8–10) and be able to meet the conditionals of his commands and promises. Biblically, God, the benefactor, offered to not only pay the debt of man's sin, but he also overcame everything that might hinder a lost person from being able to choose to accept the offer through grace enablements (John 12:35–36).[2]

Moreover, in passage after passage throughout the entirety of the Bible (several of which are included in this book), there is an undeniable portrait of people making choices between accessible options. These available options include attending consequences. In other words, unless a person is trying to prove the presence of compatibilism in these passages, no one would glean it from the wording, which graphically indicates a choice between two *accessible* options with appropriate warnings and blessings. Therefore, while it is logically possible for a person to be held responsible for what he cannot do because his inability to meet the conditional is determined, it does not seem probable, presumable, or something that is identifiably emanating from the texts we considered. This is further demonstrated by Calvinists commenting on these very passages in a libertarian manner.

Additionally, granting that it is logical for the gambler to be held responsible for this one event he cannot accomplish on his own does not entail or evidence that it is, thereby, demonstrable or even reasonable to conclude that he is to be held responsible for every other obligation but unable in every circumstance to have chosen otherwise. To clarify, someone may accept the logicalness of the gambler being held accountable in this

---

1. I first heard Leighton Flowers use this illustration at https://soteriology101.com/.

2. See Authorial Glossary for a fuller discussion of grace enablements and chapter 8 for my comments on this passage.

one case, but that does nothing to demonstrate we are to believe that leads us to conclude that it is logical for him to be unable to act in every event of his life and yet be responsible. That is the conclusion Calvinism, with its decretal theology and compatible moral freedom, ultimately demands, which I reject because it is not supported by Scripture nor life itself.

When conditional passages are read just as they are written, the understanding that emanates from the wording of the text is reflective of libertarian freedom. They are written like normal human communication that reflects real and accessible choices, which will result in different outcomes. This understanding is even evidenced by the way Calvinist commentators regularly interpret conditional passages; they do so libertarianly. While it is logically possible for someone to be held responsible for something he cannot accomplish on his own (as my illustration suggests), it seems highly implausible that all, or even many, of the conditionals in Scripture permit such an understanding. That would mean we must read countless conditional promises and events, which permeate almost every page of Scripture and include concomitant urgings, warnings, and promises by God based on whether a person meets the stated condition, as disguised deterministic passages.

The very essence of a conditional statement is that the outcome will be different depending on what choice is made, and that difference is the crux of the influence on the choice to be made. For example, a person will be saved or lost depending on his response to the gospel, and other events will have a different outcome based on whether or not a person prays; choosing can alter the future sequence of events. That is not possible in a compatible, morally free state of affairs. Compatibilism includes the voluntary principle of choice, but it excludes the possibility of choice creating a new sequence of events as libertarian freedom allows. The Scripture is replete with humans being called on to make choices based on effecting a better outcome.

Now, why would God fill Scripture with conditionals that give every reasonable appearance of being something wherein people can choose to meet or not meet, which also include understandable warnings and blessings that are inextricably connected to each choice, if he designed a plan that precluded them from actually making an undetermined choice between the options given? This in light of the inarguable reality that God does present many determined events in Scripture and is, therefore, not ashamed or clandestine about the truth that he determines some outcomes.

The Calvinist needs to explain God's purpose in being so clear about some determined events while camouflaging most of them in language that highlights obvious otherwise choice and conditionality; that is, if Calvinism is true. Their inability to satisfactorily answer this dilemma without obscuring the unambiguousness of conditional passages that permeate Scripture renders their deterministic obscurations nonsensical and Calvinism, along with its compatibilism, biblically untenable.

To clarify, Scripture is the revealing (revelation) of truths about God and his redemptive plan, rather than the obscuring of such. The grammar, context, particular sentence structure, and the clear intent which emanates from a normal reading of the conditionals is to give a person a choice of two or more accessible options. In light of this, why would God embark on such a veiling course to reveal himself and his plan? In other words, if God determined everything, then why would God give some verses that clearly teach some events are determined and equally obscure determinism in so many other verses that give every indication that events are not determined. What is the point?

Until Calvinists can make a compelling case for why God would present so many verses and entire passages involving otherwise choices in his revelation (the precise opposite of everything being determined) when they are actually clandestine deterministic events, compatibilism fosters a nonsensical option. Which, if Calvinism with its compatibilism were true, would turn revelation into obscuration and deception. If one example of otherwise choice is in Scripture (I think Scripture is permeated with examples of otherwise choice), compatibilism fails as a coherent reflection of man's moral freedom; in contrast, libertarian freedom easily accommodates both otherwise choice and determinism.

APPENDIX 2

God's Essential Omniscience Does Not Require Calvinism's Determinism

IN BOTH CALVINISM AND EXTENSIVISM, God knows all that could happen and all that will happen. The difference is in how he knows. According to Calvinism, his knowledge of what could and will happen is based upon his micro-determination.[3] Another way of saying God knows what could happen is God knows what he could determine to happen. To say it differently, God knows, out of the possibilities of what he could determine to happen, what he will determine to happen. This determinism is not merely God determining to create the universe because we all believe that creation would not exist if God did not determine to create.

Instead, Calvinism maintains that God knows what will happen, and this entails that every thought, action, and event happens only because God micro-predetermined it to be precisely as it is. His micro-determinism is accomplished by and revealed in his decrees, foreordination, and endowment of man with compatible moral freedom.[4] In this micro-determined

---

3. I am referring to mainstream consistent Decretal Calvinism, or what I often refer to as Major-Calvinism. Major-Calvinists believe in at least total depravity (Calvinistically defined), unconditional election, irresistible grace, perseverance of the saints, compatibilism, and that God predetermined everyone's eternal destiny.

4. Compatibilism is the belief that moral responsibility and determinism are compatible. Man is considered to make a free choice so long as he chooses according to his greatest desire. But it must be understood that while such choice is considered free, the desire from which it comes was determined by the individual's nature and past. While God employs secondary causes in his determination, these causes are as determined as every other determinative antecedent that results in the determined desire from which

universe, humans do not and cannot make a free choice in which the person is the efficient cause and could have chosen differently.[5] That is to say, in the moral moment of decision, humans freely choose what they were predetermined to choose, but they cannot choose differently given their same past.[6]

Extensivism argues God knows all that can and will happen because he is essentially omniscient. Therefore, God can know what he determined to happen apart from the influence of libertarian free human beings and what comes into being because of the actions and choices of libertarian free beings; the latter category is known as *contingencies*.[7] The only thing required is that God sovereignly chose to create beings with libertarian free choice. Below are seven components of what it means to be essentially omniscient.[8]

1. He knows everything

   ◻ He eternally knows everything (Ps 149:1–4; Prov 15:3; John 21:15–17). This knowledge includes even the seemingly most insignificant realities like the number of hairs on the head of each person

---

the determined free choice emanates; therefore, when we speak of God determining to create in Calvinism, it entails every aspect of creation, thereby absolutely disallowing humans to make a libertarian free otherwise choice, to choose differently than the person did, in fact, choose in the moral moment of decision.

5. Efficient cause means that we need look no further than the efficient cause to explain the cause of the event.

6. Some Calvinists, as well as other determinists, contend that God cannot know the acts of libertarian free beings, contingencies.

7. Libertarians contend determinism is not compatible with moral responsibility. Man possesses actual otherwise choice and can, therefore, act or refrain in the moral moment of decision given the same past within a given range of options; libertarianism does not require that otherwise choice be present in every situation but only some. In Christianity, God determines the range of options. Adam's range of options prior to the fall was greater than mankind's options after the fall. The range of options present prior to the fall was the result of creative grace. Fallen man can still choose between options, but the range of options is less than man had prior to the fall. This lessening includes losing the ability to make choices that are inherently righteous or spiritually restorative (making one right with God) based solely on creative grace. In order to make an inherently righteous choice or one that is spiritually restorative, God had to provision redemptive grace—grace enablements. Libertarian freedom allows for both determined events (events uninfluenced by human choice) and undetermined events (events influenced or caused by human choice) in which people choose between options. And whatever they did choose, they could have chosen differently.

8. See my book *Does God Love All or Some* for a more comprehensive comparison of the two perspectives.

who has ever lived (Matt 10:30). The reason that God knows this ever-changing reality of billions of people is not because he causes it or is necessarily going to do anything with the knowledge, but rather because he knows everything.

◦ Foreknowledge is a word that accommodates humans since God has always known everything because he is essentially omniscient. He always knew every actuality, potentiality, and what potentials he would transform into actualities. Accordingly, when we speak of God's eternal knowledge, it includes what we call foreknowledge.

2. He is *essentially* omniscient

◦ His omniscience is an essential property of his deity, which is also true of his omnipotence, omnipresence, omnibenevolence, and all other attributes and aspects of deity; therefore, he knows everything and cannot lack knowledge of anything.

3. Essential omniscience entails at least the following

◦ Nothing ever occurs to God; it cannot since there is nothing outside of his eternal knowledge that needs to become a part of his knowledge for him to know it.

◦ God does not learn perceptively, perceive knowledge. That is, he does not look outside of himself to learn or know about anything. For example, Calvinists often portray the Extensivist's perspective as if God looks down the halls of human history or something akin to looking into a crystal ball to acquire knowledge of what humans do or will do; this is a caricature with no basis.

◦ God cannot hold a false belief because he is essentially omniscient and the sum of perfection. For example, if he knows something will happen, it will happen, and he cannot be wrong.

◦ While nothing ever occurs to God, and he always knows everything at the same time, he can distinguish between the sequences of events.

◦ Essential omniscience is based upon who God is and not on what he does. To wit, his knowledge of the future is not based upon him having micro-determined everything, but, rather, it is based on him being the essentially omniscient God.

4. He knows the libertarian freewill acts of humans, which are called *contingencies*

   ◻ He knows contingencies because he *exhaustively* and *accurately* always knew he would create humans and what constitutes being human; therefore, he knows everything about them and what they can and will freely choose to do.

   ◻ As the only eternally and essentially omniscient being, he cannot become informed or be informed by anything or anyone except himself.

   ◻ As an essentially omniscient being, he cannot have incomplete knowledge of humans. Because he is essentially omniscient, that knowledge does not require determinism as its source other than his determination to create libertarian free beings. To suggest a separation between God's exhaustive knowledge of what he created as a human being and what humans would freely choose to do given an opportunity is a fallacy of artificially separating the aftereffect of God's creation from what he created. For such to be true would require the unbiblical proposition that God is not essentially omniscient because he lacks exhaustive knowledge of himself and his creation.

5. His knowledge is not *necessarily* causal

   ◻ It is a confusion of categories to conflate knowing (epistemology) with causing (etiology).[9] Although my knowledge is not perfect, infallible, or exhaustive, which means I can be wrong, it is sufficient to illustrate that causation is not intrinsic to knowing. I have always known for forty-seven years who Gina, my wife, would vote for when she goes into the voting booth. Thus far, I have never been wrong. However, that is not dependent upon me somehow causing her to vote for a particular candidate, but only because I know her well. The point of the example is not to demonstrate that I could not be wrong as is true with God but merely to show knowing does not equal causation, nor is it entailed in knowledge. To wit, determinism is one way of knowing, but it is not the only way

9. He does know some things because he determined them to exist apart from human choice, but micro-determining everything is not essential to his knowing everything as it is in Calvinism.

of knowing. Therefore, to use my fallibility to nullify the example is meritless.[10]

◻ God's foreknowledge in Calvinism is causative since Calvinism generally contends that God can know only what he determines and, therefore, denies that God can know contingencies—the acts of libertarian free beings. In contrast, God's essential omniscience entails that he knows those events that are determined (uninfluenced by human choice) and nondetermined events (influenced by or the result of human choice), which are known as contingencies.

6. He knows himself exhaustively

◻ No aspect of his being, knowledge, or the composite of all of his attributes lacks perfect exhaustive eternal knowledge.

7. He knows his intentions

◻ God has always known himself, which always includes exhaustively knowing his intentions.

◻ He always knew he intended to create humans in his image with otherwise choice (libertarian moral freedom).

◻ God's knowledge not only includes the significant counterfactual potentialities, it even includes the mundane such as knowing every sparrow that falls from the sky and the number of hairs on everyone's head (Matt 10:29–30). Both states are ever-changing and rather unimportant, yet God has eternally known everything about each of them because he is essentially omniscient. Such neither entails nor suggests he micro-causally predetermined each changing state. To separate God, knowing himself exhaustively, including his intentions, which includes his intention to create

10. Many Calvinists attempt to superimpose Calvinism's determinism on what it means for God to be essentially omniscient rather than understand the term as used by Extensivism. The attempt, although impossible, is a form of "the same problem argument" wherein Calvinists seek to palliate the harshness of the entailments of Calvinism and compatibilism by suggesting that Extensivists have the same problem as Calvinists. While each view may have problems that need to be addressed, we do not and cannot have the same problem since compatibilism and libertarianism are intrinsically opposite, and, therefore, mutually exclusive.

libertarian free beings, from knowing such beings' acts is baseless and artificial.

Therefore, he eternally and innately knew what humans would choose because he exhaustively and eternally knew himself and his intentions. He knew this without having to cause all human actions determinatively.

Authorial Glossary

Accessible Options

Options and alternatives that can actually be chosen by the persons they are given to as opposed to being merely hypothetical options in which one or both are inaccessible. By accessible options, I mean, given the same past and circumstances, the same person could choose to act or refrain or choose one option over another. Whatever he did choose to do, he could have chosen differently in the very same situation (see also Hypothetical Options).

Agency

Agency speaks of the ability of a libertarian free will being to choose, act, respond, feel, or think in a certain way for which the person is responsible; the situational circumstances may limit the range of options.

Calvinism

Some of Calvinism's core beliefs are summarized under the acronym TU-LIP 1. Total depravity; 2. Unconditional election; 3. Limited atonement; 4. Irresistible grace; 5. Perseverance of the saints. I use the term "consistent Calvinists" to refer to Calvinists who seek to speak, write, pray, and live consistent with the beliefs of actual Calvinism and its entailments; for example, that God has predetermined every thought, act, and belief so that they cannot be altered by human choice from what God determined them to be (compatibilism and decretal theology). Other entailments include such realities that God cannot be understood to salvifically love everyone (desire everyone to be saved) while maintaining (as Calvinism does) that

God withheld from them—the non-elect—the very essentials needed for them to be saved.

Certain Events

Non-determined events or outcomes that do not have to happen. They result from libertarian choice. They are only certain to happen because God knows they will, and he cannot be wrong. They are not necessary events (determined) because had the individual chosen differently, something else would have happened, and God would have known that.

Compatibilism

Determinism and moral responsibility are compatible. Free choice is when a person chooses according to his greatest desire. Given the same past, a person cannot choose differently from what he chose; he has no otherwise choice. The greatest desire from which the person freely chooses is always determined; hence, it is a determined free choice.

Conditional

A statement or command made with a stated or implied corresponding dependent outcome. The outcome is based on meeting the said condition. If you ask (condition), I will give this to you (outcome). The outcome is certain if the condition is met; if the condition is unmet, the promise is withheld. Conditionals found in biblical narratives provide examples of the prevalence, variety, and normalcy of conditionals and how they may transpire in our own lives.

Contingencies

These are events that are the result of the human choices of libertarian free beings. They are events that are non-determined. They are contingent on a libertarian free person's choice.

Counterfactual

What would have happened had a different choice been made. For example, if I had stayed home, I would not have had a car wreck driving to work.

Creation-Redemption Plan

God's coextensive plan to create and redeem man, knowing Adam and Eve would sin.

Definite Events

These are outcomes that are determined by God to happen apart from human influence. They happen necessarily.

Deliberation

◌ *Objective* deliberation is the process of libertarian free beings when considering the pros and cons of deciding between actually accessible options. Based on the person's considerations, he decides to choose one of the options and could have chosen differently. The deliberations are objective because they are *actually* related to the individual's decision, which could have been different since he is the efficient cause of his judgment (see also Efficient Cause).

◌ *Subjective* deliberation is that which a compatibly free being experiences. Experientially it feels the same as the *objective* deliberation of the libertarian free being. He believes he is choosing between *actually* accessible options even with his same past. His experience and senses tell him he could choose one option or the other and have chosen differently had he so decided. However, his deliberation is only subjective because it has no possibility of changing the predetermined choice the person will make; he only experientially senses that it does.

Determinism

I only use this term to convey determinism according to compatibilism.

Efficient Cause

The *Oxford English Dictionary* defines Efficient Cause as "an agent that brings a thing into being or indicates a change."[11] *The Oxford Guide to Philosophy* defines it as "a cause that produces something distinct from itself."[12] The *Baker Encyclopedia* tells us it moves something from potentiality to actuality. It involves the idea that one needs to look no further than the individual for the cause of the action or the event—*agent causation.*[13]

Essentially Omniscient

God is essentially omniscient, which means his knowledge of everything is an essential attribute of his being, in the same way, other essential properties of deity, like omnipotence, omnipresence, and omnibenevolence are. This is what it means to be Jehovah. He eternally knows everything; this includes actualities, potentialities, and what potentialities he would actualize.

He knows definite events because he predetermined for them to exist apart from human influence. He knows indefinite events (contingencies) because he determined to create man with libertarian freedom; as an essential property of his being, he has always known these indefinite events because he knows himself exhaustively, including his intentions, and he has always intended to create a state of affairs that included indefinite events (contingencies). He does not acquire knowledge of contingencies by looking outside of himself, down the halls of history; he does not know about contingencies, perceptively. He knows about them as an essential property of his being because he is essentially omniscient.

Extensivism

Specifically, Extensivism believes man and woman were created in the image of God with otherwise choice and God's salvation plan is comprehensive, involving an all-inclusive, unconditional offer of salvation and eternal security of the believer; reception of which is conditioned upon grace-enabled faith rather than an exclusive plan involving a limited actual offer of

11. "Efficient Cause," para. 1.

12. Honderich, *Oxford Guide*, 131.

13. Norman L. Geisler states, "So, I am the efficient cause of my own free actions, but the power of free choice is the means by which I freely act." *Baker Encyclopedia*, 220.

salvation to only the unconditionally elected, or any plan that, in any way, conditions salvation upon merely a humanly-generated faith.

Extensivism may have some things in common with Calvinism, Arminianism, or Molinism but does not rely upon any of them. Similarities do not equal sameness. Extensivism seeks only to present a comprehensive, consistent system of soteriology that is reflective of the warp and woof of Scripture. It may have shared beliefs with other systems of soteriology, but Extensivism neither relies upon nor seeks to be consistent with them.

Generally, I use Extensivism as a positive for the negative non-Calvinism.

Hypothetical Options

A hypothetical option means that if some things or something (such as the person's past, determined desires, or timing) were different, he could have chosen differently. In essence, this means in the moral moment of decision, he could not have chosen differently; thus, it is *not* an attainable or accessible option at that moment (see also Accessible Options).

Indefinite Events

Outcomes that are influenced by humans, and, therefore, not determined; they happen contingently.

Libertarianism

Determinism and moral responsibility are not compatible. Humans have otherwise choice. In some circumstances, given their same past, a person can choose differently than he did choose.

Necessary Event

Events that are determined to happen and, therefore, must happen; therefore, they happen necessarily.

Objective Will of God

This is the Scripture, which is for everyone all the time. It is the revealed will of God for everyone, everywhere, and everywhen.

Permissive Will of God

Things God allows people to do, which are not his desired best for them, and do not thwart his ultimate plan. Sin is the prime example.

Simple Approach to Scripture

I take a simple approach to the Scripture, and I am inclined to think it means what it seems to say. My approach is not a simplistic reading of Scripture because I pay attention to the grammar, the analogy of faith principle (interpreting in congruence with the rest of Scripture), the genre of the book or passage, historical context, the immediate and book context and other considerations necessary to understand the authorial intent of the passage; this is reflective of what is known as the Historical-Grammatical method. By simple, I mean I do not seek to import meaning into it. I seek to read it and see what it says, and based on what it says, I seek to understand what it means.

Subjective Will of God

God's specific or personal will for an individual, which will always be consonant with his objective will, Scripture.

Bibliography

Bergsma, Stuart. *Speaking with Tongues*. Grand Rapids: Baker, 1965.

Blum, Edwin A. "John." In *The Bible Knowledge Commentary: An Exposition of the Scriptures,* edited by J. F. Walvoord and R. B. Zuck, 2:266–346. Wheaton, IL: Victor, 1985. Logos electronic edition.

Borchert, Gerald L. *John 12–21*. The New American Commentary 25B. Nashville: Broadman & Holman, 2002.

Brooks, James A. *Mark*. The New American Commentary 23. Nashville: Broadman & Holman, 1991.

Chafer, Lewis Sperry. *Systematic Theology*. 8 vols. Grand Rapids: Kregel, 1993. Logos electronic edition.

Cole, R. Alan. "Mark." In *New Bible Commentary: 21st Century Edition*, edited by D. A. Carson et al., n.p. 4th ed. Downers Grove, IL: Inter-Varsity, 1994. Logos electronic edition.

"Efficient Cause." https://www.lexico.com/en/definition/efficient_cause.

Erickson, Millard J. *Christian Theology*. 3rd ed. 3 vols. Grand Rapids: Baker Academic, 2013.

Geisler, Norman L. *Baker Encyclopedia of Christian Apologetics*. Grand Rapids: Baker, 1999.

Grassmick, John D. "Mark." In *The Bible Knowledge Commentary: An Exposition of the Scriptures*, edited by J. F. Walvoord and R. B. Zuck, 2:102–96. Wheaton, IL: Victor, 1985. Logos electronic edition.

Grudem, Wayne. *Systematic Theology: An Introduction to Biblical Doctrine*. Grand Rapids: Zondervan, 1994.

Hagin, Kenneth. "Faith Brings Results!" https://www.rhema.org/index.php?option=com_content&view=article&id=1026:faith-brings-results&catid=46&Itemid=141.

Hanegraaff, Hank. *Christianity in Crisis*. Eugene, OR: Harvest, 1997.

Harrison, Eugene Myers. "J. Hudson Taylor: God's Mighty Man of Prayer." https://www.wholesomewords.org/missions/biotaylor3.html.

Hendriksen, William, and Simon J. Kistemaker. *Exposition of the Gospel According to Mark, New Testament Commentary, vol. 10*. Grand Rapids: Baker, 1975.

Honderich, Ted, ed. *The Oxford Guide to Philosophy*. Oxford: Oxford University Press, 2005.

Horton, Michael, ed. *The Agony of Deceit*. Chicago: Moody, 1990.

Keil, Carl Friedrich, and Franz Delitzsch. *Commentary on the Old Testament*. Vol. 1, *Pentateuch*. Peabody, MA: Hendrickson, 1996. Logos electronic edition.

BIBLIOGRAPHY

Louw, Johannes P., and Eugene Albert Nida. *Greek-English Lexicon of the New Testament: Based on Semantic Domains.* New York: United Bible Societies, 1996. Logos electronic edition.

Lowery, David K. "2 Corinthians." In *The Bible Knowledge Commentary: An Exposition of the Scriptures*, edited by J. F. Walvoord and R. B. Zuck, 2:554–85. Wheaton, IL: Victor, 1985. Logos electronic edition.

MacArthur, John. "Prayer Is Not an Attempt." *Twitter*, November 21, 2020. https://twitter.com/MastersSeminary/status/1330210615785365504?s=20.

Osteen, Joel. *Become a Better You: 7 Keys to Improving Your Life Every Day.* New York: Howard, 2007.

Peterson, John W. "I Just Keep Trusting My Lord." John W. Peterson Music, 1962.

Plummer, Alfred. *The Epistles of St. John.* 1886. Reprint, Grand Rapids: Baker, 1980.

Rogers, Ronnie W. *Does God Love All or Some: Comparing Biblical Extensivism and Calvinism's Exclusivism.* Eugene, OR: Wipf & Stock, 2019.

———. *Reflections of a Disenchanted Calvinist: The Disquieting Realities of Calvinism.* Bloomington, IN: WestBow, 2016.

Smith, Charles R. *Tongues in Biblical Perspective.* Winona Lake, IN: BMH, 1973.

Spurgeon, C. H. "Praying and Waiting." In *The Metropolitan Tabernacle Pulpit*, 10. Pasadena, TX: Pilgrim, 1969.

Subject Index

Scripture Index